Leaning Both Ways at Once

Leaning Both Ways at Once

Methodist Evangelistic Mission
at the Intersection of Church and World

Jeffrey A. Conklin-Miller

PICKWICK *Publications* · Eugene, Oregon

LEANING BOTH WAYS AT ONCE
Methodist Evangelistic Mission at the Intersection of Church and World

Pickwick Publications
An Imprint of Wipf and Stock Publishers
199 W. 8th Ave., Suite 3
Eugene, OR 97401

www.wipfandstock.com

PAPERBACK ISBN: 978-1-4982-9146-0
HARDCOVER ISBN: 978-1-4982-9148-4
EBOOK ISBN: 978-1-4982-9147-7

Cataloguing-in-Publication data:

Names: Conklin-Miller, Jeffrey A., author.

Title: Leaning both ways at once : Methodist evangelistic mission at the intersection of church and world / Jeffrey A. Conklin-Miller.

Description: Eugene, OR : Pickwick Publications, 2020 | Includes bibliographical references and index.

Identifiers: ISBN 978-1-4982-9146-0 (paperback) | ISBN 978-1-4982-9148-4 (hardcover) | ISBN 978-1-4982-9147-7 (ebook)

Subjects: LCSH: Methodist Church—Doctrines—Congresses.| Mission of the church. | Methodist Episcopal Church—Missions.

Classification: BV601.8 .C67 2020 (print) | BV601.8 .C67 (ebook)

Manufactured in the U.S.A.   AUGUST 24, 2020

Parts of chapter 3 were previously published as "'Peoplehood' and the Methodist Revival," *Wesleyan Theological Journal* 46:1 (2011): 163–82, and are reprinted with permission.

To Shannon, Emma, and Ethan

Table of Contents

TABLE OF CONTENTS

Acknowledgments

WHILE THIS PROJECT TOOK shape first as a dissertation written in the Doctor of Theology program at Duke Divinity School, in truth, it began years before that, in the form of thoughts and questions generated by my work as a pastor. I am grateful for the many conversations with all the lay and clergy colleagues inside and outside the congregations I served who helped put words to experience and perception. If I have any desire for what this book might do, it is that it add something hopeful to the formation of theological pastoral imagination. Put differently, I hope this helps pastors do the work they have been called to do.

I was blessed with the gift of time and space to return to school to pursue these questions and found at Duke Divinity School a wonderful community of teachers and colleagues. My doctoral co-advisors, Greg Jones and Laceye Warner, are to be thanked for their guidance, patience, and the ways they reminded me that I am part of the People called Methodist. I offer thanks as well to the members of my dissertation committee, Kenneth Carder, Stanley Hauerwas, and especially Randy Maddox, who has been a guide and support for many years now. I was blessed to have been a student among such faithful teachers.

Crucial support for my studies was provided by A Foundation for Theological Education and the Foundation for Evangelism through the Duke Evangelism Fellowship. Both offered not only funding but also the opportunity to share in communities of friendship and support in the form of the John Wesley and Denman Fellows, and among colleagues in the E. Stanley Jones Professors of Evangelism. I am thankful for both. Further financial support came from the Foundation of the First United Methodist Church of Escondido, California, my home church, and a congregation instrumental to my formation as a Christian, as a pastor, and a scholar. I hope for a future for the Church that reflects what makes your congregation so special.

In the past several years, many conversations with colleagues and friends at Duke Divinity School and in the broader connection of United Methodism have meaningfully shaped my ongoing thinking in this project. Thanks here especially to Randy Maddox, Laceye Warner, Edgardo Colón-Emeric, Elaine Heath, Sangwoo Kim, Kenneth Carter, Greg Moore, and Colin Yuckman. I also want to thank the many students I've had opportunity to teach (and from whom I've learned) at Duke Divinity and in the Course of Study for Local Pastors at Duke and at the Claremont School of Theology. And for sharing with me about the Changemakers Initiative, many thanks to Kim Jones and Caryn Cranston.

Relief from some administrative duties and support for research assistance helped me bring this project to completion, and for that I offer thanks to Greg Jones, Norman Wirzba, and Sujin Pak. Brent Levy offered valuable research assistance while grading papers, launching a new church, and welcoming a second child! Randy Maddox, Sangwoo Kim, Judith Heyhoe, and Shannon Conklin-Miller all read the manuscript and offered helpful feedback and guidance which improved the work. I am thankful to each for their time and effort. And finally, I'm grateful for the Epworth United Methodist Church in Durham, North Carolina and to pastors Karen Whitaker and Sangwoo Kim, who provided me access to quiet Sunday school rooms where I could write and remember what this book was always meant to be about: the ministry of the Church in the world.

Lastly, and most importantly, I want to recognize my family, whose support and love have sustained me. Especially I'm grateful to my parents, Jan and Ken, and to my in-laws, Jennifer and Bob. And to those I share life with most closely, Shannon and Emma and Ethan, I say thank you, and I give thanks for you. To each of you, in gratitude for what we have given each other and in hope for all that is still to come, I dedicate this to you.

Introduction

Next to evangelism, the most urgent task within the Christian Church—even more urgent than the much more publicized effort for ecumenicity—is the re-articulation of the Christian social ethic, of the relationship of the Christian and the church to the social order. Indeed one might well ask whether that is not essentially the evangelistic task of the day, the proclamation of a Gospel which reunites in the true New Testament sense, faith and works. . . . Such an approach of course presupposes a readiness to undergo the pre-Constantinian church-world tension and conflict.[1]

Church, World, and Wesleyan Witness

THIS PAST SUMMER, VISITORS to various cathedrals of the Church of England were treated to more than the expected spires and stained glass. For example, a site for holy travelers since the thirteenth century, Rochester Cathedral invited visitors not only to climb the historic Pilgrim Steps but also to play a round of nine holes on the newly installed miniature golf course in the nave. Farther north, the Cathedral in Norwich invited all to come and worship and, for a small fee, to take a ride down the fifty-five-foot-tall slide, also known as a "Helter Skelter."

In Norwich, the effort was part of the "Seeing it Differently" campaign, offering participants "opportunities for reflective, God-shaped conversations."[2] Such conversations also served an evangelistic purpose,

---

1. Peachey, "Toward an Understanding," 27.
2. Bryant, "Invitation," para. 2, 11.

as one of the cathedral clergy explained. To install a Helter Skelter in the cathedral is

> playful in its intent but also profoundly missional. It is the Cathedral doing what it has always done—encouraging conversations about God. By its sheer size and grandeur it speaks of the things of God; it points beyond itself. Its sheer presence helps to keep the rumour of God alive and plays its part in passing on the story of Salvation.[3]

Needless to say, not all perceived such a missional purpose. Quoted in a local newspaper, a former chaplain to the Queen panned the Norwich slide, saying,

> My real objection is that it is professional incompetence. People who are running the cathedral should understand how people are converted [to Christianity]. There is no evidence that people are converted by treating cathedrals as a cultural artefact. You want people who will come to visit because they are interested in Christianity. . . . The idea of luring people into the cathedral to have fun is stupid. . . . It is the McDonaldisation of the church.[4]

Similar divides can be heard almost annually in North American contexts as the Church nears the beginning of the Lenten season. On Ash Wednesday, several congregations see their clergy stepping outside the Church building in liturgical vestments to offer the imposition of ashes to those who have not (or will not) attend services on that day. Giving "Ashes to Go" to commuters walking by or drawing sooty crosses on the foreheads coming through the Church parking lot Ash Wednesday "drive thru," these clergy see the Church witnessing to the faith in public spaces, extending the Church's outreach and, perhaps, encouraging the congregation's numerical membership growth.[5] Others see a failure to sustain liturgical tradition and confused logic equating ashes and evangelism.[6]

Behind arguments over the propriety of miniature golf inside and the imposition of ashes outside the church building, we should acknowledge that, in one frame, what we are overhearing is an argument about the meaning and faithful practice of evangelism. As one priest commented

3. Bryant, "Invitation," para. 2, 11.

4. Powell, "Cathedral Faces Criticism," para. 5–10.

5. See "Ashes to Go"; Shaffer, "Too Busy for Church?"

6. See Conger, "Are Ashes to Go a Protestant no-no?"; Sniffen, "Ashes to Go or Not to Go."

when considering the cathedral initiatives, "We are faced with a missionary situation of trying to connect people with the transcendent when we know from British social attitudes, people have given up on it."[7] Similar dynamics exist in the United States, where the Pew Research Center suggests that 61 percent of Americans report as either somewhat or non-religious.[8] This latter category, the non-religious or "religious 'nones'" has been steadily growing, particularly in younger generations.[9] Paired with research that suggests a general decline in the membership and involvement in American congregations, ecclesial interest in empowering outreach and recruitment seems understandable, if not mandatory.[10] In turn, disagreements over the proper shape of that outreach seem inevitable.

What is striking about such reflection is the stark differentiation of judgment at work: one person's faithful and hopeful evangelistic mission is another's dismal and sinful ecclesial failure.[11] It might come as little surprise that there is a spectrum of different judgments on this question among the various theological traditions in contemporary Christianity. But there is also divergence *within* individual traditions. Most specifically, within the Wesleyan tradition—which will be at the center of this study—Jack Jackson has drawn attention to three major distinct frameworks adopted in Wesleyan academic understandings of evangelism: proclamation, initiation, and embodiment.[12] While complementary, these frameworks differ from one another regarding the scope and the focus of evangelism's concern,

7. Specia, "God Save the Cathedral?," para. 15.

8. Alper, "From the Solidly Secular," para. 3.

9. Lipka, "Closer Look," para. 3.

10. Sociologist Mark Chaves reports that "involvement in American religious congregations has softened over recent decades. Aggregate weekly attendance at worship services is either stable or very slowly declining since 1990, but it clearly declined in the decades before that, and the percent of people who never attend is steadily increasing. Moreover, each new cohort of individuals attends religious services less than did earlier cohorts at the same age, and each new generation of Americans is less likely to be raised in a religiously active family than were earlier generations" (Chaves, "Decline of American Religion?," 3).

11. With the term "evangelistic mission," I mean to bring attention to evangelism's location inside the broader frame of the *missio Dei*, God's creative, redemptive, reconciling activity throughout all creation. With such a placement, I show agreement with Dana Robert, who has argued that "the relationship of evangelism to mission is like the relationship of the heart to the body" (Robert, "Evangelism as the Heart of Mission," 4). The term "evangelistic mission" hopefully keeps this relationship before us.

12. Jackson, *Offering Christ*, xii–xiv.

as well as the identity and the agency of the Church in the practice. This constitutes, in Jackson's words, an "imprecise mosaic of understandings of evangelism."[13] That said, it could be imagined that different positions on the definition of evangelism might lead to different positions regarding the faithful shape of the Church's outreach: for some, this is constituted in ministry focused on the proclamation of the gospel, for others, on ecclesial practices of formation and initiation, and still for others, on the ethical embodiment of the gospel in diverse expressions and contexts. Still, in spite of shared commitments, there would be enough difference at work to render debate over amusement rides in the sanctuary or ashes in congregational parking lots.

For example, Scott Jones considers similar questions and challenges briefly in his book, *The Evangelistic Love of God and Neighbor*. Quoting Dana Robert, Jones observes that "fixing upon a balance between contextualization and remaining faithful to the core of the gospel is an ongoing issue in missiology."[14] His own approach to engage this issue displays a distinctively Wesleyan character, grounded in a commitment to the universal love of God for all creation, focused in the gift of the Incarnation. Jones writes, "Since Christ is God put into human flesh, the gospel can be put into other languages and cultural forms."[15] Christians, then, are called to love not only people, but also the cultures within which they live, and so moved by this love, the Church's practice of evangelism becomes crucially important.

Jones does consider the critique of market-driven evangelism as well as those who champion such techniques for the sake of Church growth.[16] While one side calls for the distinctiveness of the Church's witness and the other for the Church's adaptation seeking its relevance in every context, Jones asks whether perhaps "both are partially right?"[17] To chart a path between their divergent concerns, Jones emphasizes the importance of discipleship, rightly recognizing that the Church is called to faithfulness within a context that is always local. Given this particularity, the practice of discernment inside an account of discipleship becomes even more

---

13. Jackson, *Offering Christ*, xiv.

14. Jones, *Evangelistic Love of God and Neighbor*, 121.

15. Jones, *Evangelistic Love of God and Neighbor*, 124.

16. Jones, *Evangelistic Love of God and Neighbor*, 128–32.

17. Jones, *Evangelistic Love of God and Neighbor*, 131.

important, inasmuch as "the determination of context is a complex matter of judgment."[18]

Despite this complexity, Jones displays confidence in the possibility of faithful evangelism engaging context when he suggests that the congregation must identify a "particular target population" and then must "love the members of that group as well."[19] The shape of that love certainly informs practices of hospitality and welcome as well as concern for the "physical needs and justice issues in the community."[20] But Jones argues that evangelistic outreach also requires the Church's willingness to change in the process of becoming more visible to the community. "Christians today must adapt to the dominant modes of communication in a digital age," Jones suggests.[21] Further programming is necessary in congregations to ensure the presence of "indigenous worship," an "appropriate communications system to invite persons to know Christ," and a "system of discipleship" to form new Christians.[22] Other strategies and tactics Jones names complete a helpful list for congregations seeking to strengthen their evangelistic outreach.[23]

On this basis, perhaps Jones would not rule out the possibility of a Helter Skelter in the Cathedral's nave, just to the extent such an initiative reflects the fruit of discernment of the needs and desires in that particular context. But it is just at this point that I want to draw attention and name a problem for further consideration.

Beyond these questions relating to the tactical propriety of various innovations and differentiated understandings of evangelism's ends, I think there is more going on here. These examples of (and debates over the shape of) missional evangelism reveal other questions that lie closer to the heart of the identity and the agency of the Church and of the world where it is located. In other words, what appears to be a question about evangelism is, at a deeper level, a more fundamental question: how shall we understand the differentiation and relationship between the Church and the world?

While Jones's suggestions for congregational development are constructive, and while he is right to point to the importance of discipleship as

18. Jones, *Evangelistic Love of God and Neighbor,* 132.

19. Jones, *Evangelistic Love of God and Neighbor,* 195–96.

20. Jones, *Evangelistic Love of God and Neighbor,* 194–96.

21. Jones, *Evangelistic Love of God and Neighbor,* 198.

22. Jones, *Evangelistic Love of God and Neighbor,* 198, 200–201, 203.

23. Jones, *Evangelistic Love of God and Neighbor,* 191–203.

crucial to an account of evangelism, I fear he may understate the tensions inherent in the Church's navigation of the world in evangelistic mission. How, for example, does discipleship ensure the Church's balance between faithfulness and relevance? When the Church leans into the world, how far is too far? A miniature golf course or an amusement park ride in the cathedral crosses the line for some, while for others, it represents missional faithfulness. Presumably, discipleship shaping evangelistic mission requires a discerning judgment that determines the Church's "Yes" and "No," responding in each context to what the Church can reflect and what it must renounce. But what is less clear is what conditions make such judgment possible? What kind of community is capable of this discernment? What challenges does this community face from the world that surrounds it?

These are important questions that have not received adequate attention in the study of evangelism. This may be the case because such questions may appear to be more naturally located in other disciplinary contexts. The theological relationship, and more specifically, the theological distinction of the Church and the world, is a topic typically located not in the theology of evangelism, but rather, in ecclesial ethics. Even so, in this book, I will suggest the central role such a theological frame must play in contemporary theology and practice of evangelism. Working from this theological frame, we will be able to speak of the Church and the world in terms that acknowledge their distinct identities and agencies, and thus, create the conditions necessary to discern the faithful shape of the Church's evangelistic mission in and with the world.

While the Church-World relationship and distinction (to which I will refer henceforth in shorthand as simply "Church/World") is a theological commitment most recognizable within the Anabaptist-Mennonite tradition, the concern for the relationship of Church/World (and, at times, a lack of concern for that relationship) is just as crucial to an account of a Wesleyan understanding of holiness, and thus, to an account of Methodist identity in ecclesiology and evangelistic mission. In order then to develop a theology of evangelism that is also truly Methodist, engagement with the distinct identity and agencies associated with the Church and the world is also required. For example, this distinction is crucial if the practice of evangelism participates in the formation of what a Wesleyan would call holiness of heart and life. If holiness at least names the difference Christian identity and practice makes, then concern for this difference should play a constitutive role in an account of how such Christian identity is formed and how Christian practices take their shape.

I will suggest that this focus on holiness contributes to an ecclesiological vision that renders Church in the Methodist tradition in the form of a particular "People" in, but not of, the world. In other words, Methodist evangelistic mission requires a location within an account of ecclesiology that is framed within the Church/World distinction. So framed, the agency of the Church's witness can be articulated in terms that carve a path between ecclesial accommodation for the sake of cultural relevance in the world (what I will call "understatement") and ecclesial self-absorption that grounds Christian witness in an aesthetic display to the world (what I will call "overstatement"). Instead, the Church as a visible, practicing, and witnessing People appear as a community constantly engaging both the practices of intra-ecclesial formation and extra-ecclesial engagement with the "other half of the reconciling event" in the world.

This engagement constitutes an expansion of what we mean by the word "evangelism," as the People called Methodist practice "intercession" in and for the world. Evangelism as intercession suggests practices beyond sole concern for individual spiritual salvation or congregational membership growth. While it certainly includes the proclamation of the gospel, the initiation of people into the Church (or, for some, the reign of God), and the formation of a holy People, evangelism as intercession requires a broader scope. As Stephen Chapman and Laceye Warner have rightly argued, "The concept of evangelism should . . . be expanded to include the entire *missio Dei* of global reconciliation, particularly through the *imitatio Dei* of God's people in their care for creation and all its creatures. Social justice, peace, and ecological concern are not beyond the scope of evangelism."[24] In my terms, this is the work of a People called Methodist, practicing intercession as they stand between formation and mission, between tradition and innovation, between God and the world, always *leaning both ways at once*.

"Counterweighting" Church and World: Leaning Both Ways at Once

The image of a simultaneous "leaning both ways" is drawn from the concept of a "counterweighting," revealed in an unlikely set of sources. First, the

24. Chapman and Warner, "Jonah and the Imitation of God," 43. See also Warner, *Saving Women*.

poet Seamus Heaney in his collection of essays, *The Redress of Poetry*, suggests that poetry can fulfill what he calls a "counterweighting" function,[25] offering a "glimpsed alternative" of life that is often "denied or constantly threatened by circumstances."[26] Poetry, in this light, offers the possibility of forming a "consciousness [that] can be alive to two different and contradictory dimensions of reality and still find a way of negotiating between them."[27] Heaney draws these images from Simone Weil—specifically *Gravity and Grace*—and argues that Weil's work is "informed by the idea of counterweighting, of balancing out the forces, of redress—tilting the scales of reality toward some transcendent equilibrium."[28] It is in this counterweighting, this "tilting," that Weil seeks to inhabit as the tensioned space between gravity and grace, between the "contradictories" of this world.

However, for Weil, life between the "contradictories" does not seek to deflate the tension endemic to that space; as she writes, "The union of contradictories involves a wrenching apart. It is impossible without extreme suffering. The correlation of contradictories is detachment."[29] Instead, Weil poignantly suggests that this tilting requires a "simultaneous existence of incompatible things in the soul's bearing; [a] balance which leans both ways at once." That, Weil says, "is saintliness."[30]

In other words, what Weil is suggesting is that we do not try to "solve" what we have come to think of as fixed and opposing "contradictories"—relevance and irrelevance, tradition and mission, Church and world. Rather, in *Gravity and Grace*, she invites us to inhabit the tense space between supposed polarities without giving into the need to eliminate or even alleviate the anxiety and paradox endemic to that location "in between." Weil invites us to dwell in that intersection, and with that invitation, offers an image to shape ecclesial identity and evangelistic mission; between these polarities, we seek a balance that leans both ways at once, into the Church and into the world.

25. Jones, "Practice of Christian Governance," 117.

26. Heaney, *Redress of Poetry*, 3–4. I am indebted to Jones, "Practice of Christian Governance," 117, who mentions Heaney.

27. Heaney, *Redress of Poetry*, xiii.

28. Heaney, *Redress of Poetry*, xiii; Weil, *Gravity and Grace*, 92.

29. Weil, *Gravity and Grace*, 92.

30. Weil, *Gravity and Grace*, 92.

The Structure of the Argument

We will begin in chapter 1 with consideration of the Church/World distinction, first investigating its necessity in conversations about evangelism and then seeking its influence (or lack thereof) in contemporary Wesleyan theology of evangelism. We will find that the Church/World distinction is often understated or overstated, sometimes collapsing one into the other, or distancing one from the other.

In constructing an account of ecclesial evangelism, we turn to consider the identity and the agency of the world in chapter 2, drawing focus to the formative influence of the principalities and powers. This should come as some surprise, inasmuch as I will also show Wesley's strong warning to Methodists to navigate their relationship with the world with care. Given the consideration of the identity and the agency of the powers mediated through the example of the modern market-state, I argue for the crucial role of intra-ecclesial formation within contemporary Methodist theology of evangelistic mission.

Pursuing the development of such an account, the final two chapters turn to consider the identity (chapter 3) and the agency (chapter 4) of the Church inside the Church/World framework, oriented toward developing an account of ecclesial evangelism. In the third chapter, I suggest that Methodism is best understood as a "People called Methodist," a movement for individual and social reform that requires location in a visible, practicing, and witnessing community of discipleship. Such Peoplehood constitutes the basis for a missional ecclesiology that embodies a set of evangelistic practices and structures aimed at shaping transformed lives and a transformed world, leaning into the traditions and practices of the Christian tradition as well as into the needs of the world, both ways at once.

Chapter 4 builds on this account of a Methodist peoplehood to suggest that a Methodist People is not only shaped in the practice of the General Rules, but also, at the same time, in that People's ongoing evangelistic engagement with the world. Put differently, a Methodist Peoplehood is constantly "appearing" and is "discovered" as it takes shape at the intersection of Church/World. This engagement is best understood as the evangelistic agency of a Methodist People, described and embodied as the practice of "intercession," the Church standing between God and the world, leaning both ways at once. The implications of such an understanding shapes imagination to envision a People practicing an intercessory evangelism in initiatives and programs, institutions and structures, that are simultaneously larger than and smaller than the contemporary congregation. We will consider some of these embodiments in a brief conclusion.

The Hope for This Work

In his foreword to the re-release of Julian Hartt's book, *Toward a Theology of Evangelism*, Stanley Hauerwas suggests that to find a book about evangelism written by a theologian might come as a surprise. This is the case, he says, because

> for some time those concerned about evangelism, as well as those writing about it, have not been theologians. They have been sociologists or people that specialize in marketing . . . [and] if the church is to recover a proper sense of evangelism, that is, an understanding of evangelism that is not equated with church growth then a book about evangelism written by a theologian will be a crucial resource.[31]

This study exists as a contribution to the conversation about the ecclesial identity and the practice of evangelistic mission in the Methodist tradition, and particularly, The United Methodist Church in North America. Even though this study arrives at a moment of division and potentially the fracture of United Methodism, I offer it as an engagement in these conversations with an unmistakable concern for the development of a robustly Wesleyan theological voice in the determination of ecclesial identity and evangelistic mission. To that end, I hope that it joins many others emerging in this field, to serve together as "crucial resources" in this important conversation. How can we continue to speak into the intricate work of discerning the particular needs, the possible adhesions, necessary renunciations, and potential alliances in the textured space where pastors and congregations, where leaders and institutions, where Christians live—namely, at the intersection of Church and world? Our work in answering this question begins now.

31. Hauerwas, "Foreword."

1

Evangelism, Church, and World

Evangelism is a practice that is performed at boundaries and along the edges of difference. Because of that, nothing could be more important to a theology of evangelism than clarifying the nature of that difference and . . . the Christian community's posture toward the world along those boundaries.[1]

Mission is certainly not just the exercise of a kind of hyperactive communications strategy. But neither is it simply sitting, and hoping somebody might notice.[2]

Introduction

IN THIS CHAPTER, I will consider the means by which the theological relationship, and more specifically, the theological distinction, between the Church and the world plays a role in a theology of evangelism. This distinction is crucial if the practice of evangelism participates in the formation of what a Wesleyan would call "holiness of heart and life."[3] If holiness at least

1. Stone, *Evangelism after Christendom*, 172.

2. Williams, "God's Mission and Ours," 2.4.

3. In his "Advice to the People Called Methodists," John Wesley clarifies this term when he writes, "By Methodists I mean a people who profess to pursue (in whatsoever measure they have attained) holiness of heart and life, inward and outward conformity to the revealed will of God; who place religion in an uniform resemblance of the great

names the difference Christian identity and practice makes, then concern for this difference should play a constitutive role in an account of how such Christian identity is formed and how Christian practices take their shape at the intersection of Church/World.

As a step toward developing such an account, first we must ask, "Why employ the frame of 'Church/World?'" What is it about that particular theological construction that becomes so important for a conversation in the theology of evangelism? A concern for the Church's identity and agency vis-à-vis the world is to raise questions in the domain of ecclesiology and ethics, and such an engagement, as I suggest in this book, is crucial to developing an account of evangelism. In other words, to draw a focus on the Church and the world demands accounts of each, their relationship, and what faithful evangelistic practice might look like at that intersection.

Why the Distinction of Church and World?

In conversations about the theology and practice of ecclesial renewal, congregational development, and the "missional church," the practice of evangelism continues to inhabit troubled space. Given long-standing divisions in North American Christianity, rooted in developments in the late nineteenth and early twentieth centuries, embodied and described in a variety of dualisms ("modernists versus fundamentalists, liberals versus conservatives, and social gospelers versus personal gospelers," for example), evangelism became understood as a practice primarily concerned "to shape individual convictions," while "social action" came to describe Christian "direct action aimed at changing the social structure to bring about social justice."[4]

Such divisions have played significant roles in the twentieth-century ecumenical conversation concerning the relationship between the evangelistic proclamation of the gospel and the Church's participation in ministries seeking social justice in the world. As Norman Thomas notes, following the insights of David Bosch, "The focus of the church's mission during the first three decades of [the twentieth] century was on *evangelism*."[5] From that

---

Object of it; in a steady imitation of him they worship in all his imitable perfections; more particularly in justice, mercy, and truth, or universal love filling the heart and governing the life" (Wesley, "Advice," §2, *Works*, 9:123–24).

4. Schmidt, *Souls*, xxx–xxxi.

5. Thomas, "Ecumenical Directions," 52–63.

time forward, Thomas argues, stretching from the ecumenical gathering at Tambaram in 1938 to the meeting of the World Council of Churches (WCC) at New Delhi in 1961, "the *church* was the primary focus," presumably as the final destination toward which evangelistic efforts were all aimed.[6] Indeed, this was part of the reason for the founding of the WCC in 1948, namely, "to support the churches in their worldwide missionary and evangelistic tasks."[7] But Thomas notes that the ground had moved by 1961, with the gathering in New Delhi, where a discernible shift of emphasis was placed on the world "as the primary focus for God's concern."[8] Yet, as John Howard Yoder argued, the division between evangelism and social witness has roots more deeply planted in the history of the Reformation, as some place hope for renewal in a transformed spiritual life, others in the broader development of a holy society, divided by differing accounts of where the center of "historical meaning" is located.[9]

But Yoder introduces an interesting problem at just this point. He argues that because differing traditions of renewal locate historical meaning in different places, they cannot, finally, find peace with one another, which results in an endless "oscillation" in the Church between spiritual renewal and social renewal. What is necessary, then, is the grounding of both forms of renewal in a more primary location for historical meaning, namely, in the "People of God." The identification of the Church as a particular "People" offers an ecclesiological identity that is instructive to an account of evangelistic mission. Bryan Stone, for example, drawing on these insights, claims that "Christian evangelism requires as a condition of its very possibility the presence in the world, though distinct from the world, of a visible people, a new society, into which persons may be invited and formed."[10] However, because the Church has lost much of this sense of its own identity and mission in the world, Stone rightly suggests that this "neglect of Peoplehood may well be the central challenge facing Christian evangelism."[11]

The possibility for such a Peoplehood is premised on a theological understanding of the differentiation of Church/World. For Yoder, and thus, for Stone, that which is world is still God's creation, but it is a part

6. Thomas, "Ecumenical Directions," 52–63.

7. Thomas, "Ecumenical Directions," 52–63.

8. Thomas, "Ecumenical Directions," 52–63.

9. Yoder, "People in the World," 65–101.

10. Stone, *Evangelism after Christendom*, 194–95.

11. Stone, *Evangelism after Christendom*, 194–95.

of creation that is distinguished from the Church not in orders of being, but rather by virtue of its resistance to the confession that Jesus is Lord. In Yoder's words, "Church and world are not two compartments under separate legislation or two institutions with contradictory assignments, but two levels of pertinence of the same Lordship."[12] Of significant importance here is not just the fact of the Church/World distinction, but to be more precise, the nature of that differentiation—rooted not in ontology or geography, but rather, in agency. This is to say that while the Church and the world are both part of creation, and thus, historically located, embedded in time and space, they are to be differentiated by the trajectories they travel or the aims they seek. Again, to echo Yoder, the difference is that the Church acknowledges in its life and, thus, in its way of life, its agency—the Lordship of Jesus. The world does not.

I will reflect on the character of the differentiated agencies of Church and world in subsequent chapters. Both must be considered along the way to the construction of an ecclesiology that emphasizes the evangelistic witness embodied in the holiness of the Church, a people "in but not of" the world. For now, the question that we must answer is this: why is this consideration of the Church/World difference so crucial for an account of evangelism? There are three reasons.

First, without an account of the differentiation of Church/World, we lose the capacity to speak theologically about the mission of the Church and, thus, of the practice of evangelism. For Yoder, this differentiation sets the terms of what constitutes the Church's mission in the world. He writes, "The people of God is called to be today what the world is called to be ultimately."[13] In other words, the mission of the people of God is dependent on an account of the distinction of the Church and the world, inasmuch as it is in the Church that the world rediscovers its vocation. For Wesleyans, the distinction is best understood in terms of holiness, the sanctification of Christians and the Church that renders the Church as distinct from the world and at the same time fuels the Christian and the Church's evangelistic mission aimed at serving the world. Without a concern for the content and formation of holiness, a concern for the distinction of the Church and the world also suffers, and in turn, so does the hope for a meaningful account of evangelistic mission. Rowan Williams acknowledges a similar commitment: "If we are to keep on learning about Christ, then at the very least the

12. Yoder, *Body Politics*, ix.
13. Yoder, *Body Politics*, ix.

Church needs practices, conventions and life-patterns that keep alive the distinctiveness of the Body. . . . To use the heavily loaded language common in these discussions; a church which does not at least possess certain features of a 'sect' cannot act as an agent of transformation."[14]

Of course, care must be exercised in articulating the nature of this distinction that the formation holiness underwrites, particularly to avoid what I will describe below as the potential under-and overstatement of the Church/World distinction. David Bosch, reflecting on this dynamic at the beginning of his landmark study, *Transforming Mission*, writes that "neither a secularized church . . . nor a separatist church . . . can faithfully articulate the *missio Dei*."[15] Instead, he proposes that for meaningful mission, the Church can only exist "living in" what he calls, "the *creative tension* of, at the same time, being called out of the world and sent into the world."[16] Such a distinction, properly understood, does not undermine a robust account of ecclesial mission; instead, it makes such an account possible.

Second, beyond underwriting the mere possibility of a theological account of evangelistic mission, attention to the distinction of Church/World prevents the potential distortion of such an account. Such distortions can lead to negative outcomes in contexts of evangelistic practice. For instance, without adequate reflection on the Church's agency, the Church's identity can be reductively described in instrumental terms. While the Church is sometimes described as an instrument (often alongside other descriptions such as "foretaste" and "sign" of the Kingdom of God), this is not to say that the Church is simply a "tool" for evangelism (often understood as "church growth"). Without care for the distinction of Church/World, we lose sight of what we mean when we speak of the Church, and the ways in which only the Church can be called to pursue these practices we name as evangelism.

At the same time, without this reflection on agency, we risk overstating the Church's responsibility for evangelistic witness, to the end that the Church fails to take seriously its own tendency to sin. The close relationship between evangelistic mission and some of the Church's most problematic practices in history (colonial domination, violent crusades, endorsing slavery) must always give us pause. A lack of reflection on and confession of the Church's failures and sins in utilizing its agency impedes the crucial memory necessary to rightly identify evangelism firstly as the work of the

14. Williams, *On Christian Theology*, 233.

15. Bosch, *Transforming Mission*, 11.

16. Bosch, *Transforming Mission*, 11 (emphasis mine).

triune God in and through the Church. Thus, reflection on the Church's agency is not only reflection on what the Church "does," but also what it is called to do to remember that it is not God. In this way, a focus on the distinction of Church/World helps the Church to see the crucial role the practices of confession and repentance play in the discernment and embodiment of faithful evangelistic mission.

Such reflection on ecclesial agency creates the conditions necessary for the theological description of the world, and particularly the ways in which God has given the world a certain agency. As we will see in chapter 2, the world as conceived in biblical witness is most certainly part of God's creation and is called "good." These "principalities and powers" in their original created state are established by God for a certain purpose, in service to the God who created them. Yet, as we will see, in their fallenness, these powers and principalities have turned from God's aim to serve their own disobedient purposes. So rendered, the world is not a neutral party, but instead, has a particular agency, aimed not at serving the will of God, or reflecting the ways of Jesus, but rather, directed to its own ends, which (again, as we will see more clearly in chapter 2) are defined as survival and self-aggrandizement. However, if the world is not allowed to be "the world" understood in these terms, what does the Church risk when witnessing to the fallen world? What effect might this have on the witness of the Church? Indeed, without this reflection on agency, the world in theologies of evangelism is often rendered in neutral terms, as "culture" or "context" from which the Church is able to borrow at will for the sake of the translation and the apologetic communication of the gospel. In the atheological reading of the world, the distinction collapses and the Church too easily leans so far into the world as to fall in, losing itself in the process.

This points to the third reason why this consideration of the Church/World distinction is so crucial, namely because it creates the conditions necessary to imagine the shape of Christian practice acknowledging the complexity endemic to the discernment of faithful life in the world. As one can imagine, embodied life at the intersection of Church/World constitutes a complicated existence in time. Engagement in the life of the local Church confirms this, as it is a community constantly living in the tensions between maintaining identity and seeking intelligibility, conserving tradition and embracing innovation. To ignore these questions of agency leads to a privileging of one pole of these tensions over the other, resulting in reflections on practice that tend to deflate the tensions and, consequently, negatively impact the possibility of theologically informed, faithful practice. An account of formation without evangelistic mission is a move toward sectarianism, and an account of evangelistic mission without formation is a move toward capitulation, the Church's unquestioning translation of the gospel. Concern for both is concern for maintaining the balance between supporting the Church's traditioned identity and the Church's missional intelligibility. Consideration of the agencies of Church/World is crucial to such practical theological reflection.

Church/World and Methodist Theology of Evangelism

Despite the argument here, however, such consideration is often missing in contemporary Methodist theologies of evangelism. In his 1971 Denman Lectures, published as *Evangelism in the Wesleyan Spirit*, Albert Outler offers some description of the fractured nature of evangelistic theology and practice.[17] He argues that evangelism in the late twentieth century suffered under the stereotypes it inherited from early American revival experiences embodied in the First and Second Great Awakenings. From the first, fueled by the preaching of Jonathan Edwards (among others, including George Whitefield), Outler argues that evangelism came to focus on "a personal experience of deliverance from the wrath to come, and of God's unmerited mercy."[18] Despite the inclusion of a God of grace at the end of his description of this evangelistic practice, Outler makes his judgment clear: "It was an evangelism rooted largely in terror."[19] So framed, evangelism in this era takes conversion to be its primary end, focused on the "decisive change of heart and mind and will," a conversion "from despair to trust," and all this understood to take place within the life of the solitary individual.[20]

The problematic equation of evangelism with conversion tied to a growing commitment to individualism came to full bloom in the Second Great Awakening. This affected not only the shape of evangelistic practice, but also the theological framework that gave it meaning, inasmuch as Outler sarcastically puts it, the practice of evangelism tends to eschew "the niceties of theological distinctions and church formalities."[21] Instead, he ar-

17. Outler, *Evangelism.*
18. Outler, *Evangelism,* 58.
19. Outler, *Evangelism,* 57.
20. Outler, *Evangelism,* 58.
21. Outler, *Evangelism,* 58.

gues, evangelism came to be associated with a very narrow set of theological concerns, including an anthropomorphic vision of God, an Eutychian Christology (emphasizing Christ's human nature absorbed and dominated by his divine nature), and substitutionary atonement lifted up as the proper and solitary understanding of Christ's saving work, all of which funded primary focus on justification-as-salvation while neglecting sanctification and the ongoing formation of holy living. Here again, conversion was posited as the telos of evangelistic outreach, and not as the beginning of a life of discipleship.

Yet, for Outler, this is not only where evangelism loses connection to a broader, and presumably more faithful, set of traditional theological commitments; it is also the place that evangelism ceases to be authentically Wesleyan. He argues that Wesley firmly held to the belief that "conversion is never more than the bare threshold of authentic and comprehensive evangelism."[22] Thus, for Wesley, and in contrast to developments in American Methodist evangelistic practice, Outler suggests that "sanctification became the goal and end of all valid evangelistic endeavor," which, he adds, beyond the immediacy of conversion, "implies a lifelong process."[23] Thus, an authentically Wesleyan evangelism must move beyond the limited vision of the Great Awakenings, and "rediscover . . . that evangelism barely begins with conversion and a profession of faith," but instead, "must always lead beyond to a lifelong mission of witness and service in the world for which Christ died."[24] Put simply, a more authentic Wesleyan evangelism requires a closer relationship between justification and sanctification.

But for Outler, Wesleyan evangelism also demands more than the reunification of justification and sanctification. Given his articulation of Methodist ecclesiological identity and evangelistic mission nearly a decade earlier in his address to the Oxford Institute for Methodist Theological Studies in 1962, it comes as no surprise that in his Denman Lectures, Outler similarly argues for a reconnection of evangelism and Methodist ecclesial identity.[25] In short, he envisions Methodist evangelism to be the practice of the Church, the witness of a sanctified community of witnesses to the world. In his words, "evangelism is never a private affair: it is the outreaching hand and heart of the *People* of God, drawing men [sic] into

22. Outler, *Evangelism*, 23.

23. Outler, *Evangelism*, 23.

24. Outler, *Evangelism*, 32.

25. Outler, "Do Methodists Have a Doctrine of the Church?"

the fellowship of faith and grace."[26] Thus, Wesleyan evangelism must always begin and end with "visible social effects;" the word made audible must become the word made visible.[27]

At first glance, there may be little that seems novel in this configuration. To the extent that the church is defined as a gathering of faithful disciples, it may already appear settled that the church is therefore the logical location for evangelistic practice. But I suggest there is more going on here. Outler argues that the gathering of Societies and the practices of sacramental piety and community discipline were not simply the "next stage" movements in Christian discipleship formation following an evangelistic practice that began with proclamation and ended with an individual's conversion. Even more, these practices constituted the Methodists as not only a gathering of holy people, but as a "People" who put holiness on display—a visible, practicing, Christian community, which locates its evangelistic proclamation in the embodied witness of its life offered to the world. Such witness is the "outer effect" made evident to the world when the Church is constituted as a community of "martyrs and servants."[28]

With this focus on the evangelistic nature of the Church itself, Outler takes a step beyond an instrumental ecclesiology, rendering Church only as the geographic location of or the inert container for evangelistic practice. Instead, Outler draws attention to the Church not only as the context of evangelistic practice, but also as an agent in the practice of evangelism. While it would be wrong to ascribe to Outler an overt concern for the distinction of Church and world, it is notable that what we do find in his account of evangelism is a strong affirmation of the Church's identity and agency, a reconnection of evangelism to ecclesiology, considering the relationship of ecclesial identity to ecclesial witness.

Subsequent Methodist theological reflection on the shape of evangelism continued to reflect Outler's concern for a holistic soteriology (keeping justification and sanctification, conversion and discipleship, tightly connected), as well as his interest in the identity and role of the Church in the practice. Perhaps more clearly stated is the placement of these concerns in a broader eschatological frame, adding reflection on and implication for the identity and agency of the Church and the world in the practice of evangelism.

26. Outler, *Evangelism*, 53.

27. Outler, *Evangelism*, 101.

28. Outler, *Evangelism*, 84–109.

Of particular note here are the contributions of Mortimer Arias and William Abraham in the 1980s, both of whom draw focus to the centrality of eschatology in a theology of evangelism. Somewhat similarly, Arias argues for an evangelism embodying the eschatological "announcement" of the Reign of God, while Abraham defines evangelism as "primary initiation into the Kingdom of God."[29] The move is crucial for both in the sustaining offer of evangelism with a holistic character, holding together concern for proclamation and action, justification and sanctification, conversion and formation in a life of discipleship.

What is not as clearly connected in these offers is consideration of the identity and agency of both Church and the world in evangelism. While Arias and Abraham each ground a theology of evangelism in eschatology, they tend to underemphasize one half of the Church/World relationship. In Arias, we find acknowledgement of the principalities and the powers in the world to whom the proclamation of the Kingdom of God must be aimed. But lacking more developed ecclesiological reflection, it is not always clear in Arias who practices this proclamation. In Abraham, the issue is inverted. He rightly names Church as one of the "agents" in the practice of evangelism, and more than most, offers greater reflection on the identity and character of this ecclesial agency. Yet, unlike Arias, we do not find as developed a consideration of the focus of evangelistic ministry, as Abraham speaks of the agency of the "unevangelized" and not the world. Brief consideration of both will display the contributions they make toward a theology of evangelism that "leans both ways at once."

For Arias, evangelism echoes the "announcement" of the Reign of God in Jesus Christ. In an acknowledgement of the agency of the world, Arias argues that the Kingdom that Jesus announces in his life and ministry is a Kingdom that is "confrontational" to a world that finds the offer of Jesus's new inclusive community to be a threat. Thus, Arias concludes, "as we see it in the Gospels, then, the coming of the Kingdom means a permanent confrontation of worlds."[30] This means that while the shape of evangelism might take the form of "gift" and "hope" offered by the Church to the world, it must also be ready to take on the identity of being a "challenge" to the world as well.[31] Specifically, evangelism must sometimes take the form of what Arias calls "denunciation." Here, evangelism

29. Arias, *Announcing the Reign*, 79; Abraham, *Logic of Evangelism*, 13.

30. Arias, *Announcing the Reign*, 46.

31. These constitute the themes for chapters 6, 7, and 8 in Arias, *Announcing the Reign*.

takes the shape of prophetic denunciation of personal and public sin; of confrontation of powers and institutions; of unmasking ideologies and traditions; of challenge to unbelief, prejudice, and hostility; and of challenge also to triumphalistic belief. Finally, it takes the form of repentance, conversion, and radical discipleship.[32]

Anything less than this results in a theology and practice of evangelism that falls short of witness to the Kingdom of God and functions instead as a form of propaganda.[33]

Arias also considers the shape of the body that practices this eschatological embodiment of evangelism. Here, he articulates a call to "recover the communal dimension of the church—and of evangelization," and finally ties this call to the "great and unique resources in the local churches," where "a holistic announcement of the kingdom can take place as the natural projection of the local church in proclamation, fellowship, celebration, teaching and learning, and service."[34] He seems to also to suggest that such an announcement of God's reign will require ecclesial agency that leans both ways at once: "We need both the prophetic distance from any particular order and the freedom to engage ourselves with the rest of society to work for the common good."[35] In other words, Arias is calling for engagement with the complicated question of the Church's differentiation from and engagement with the world in evangelism.

While this call moves in positive directions, however, Arias leaves the theme of the Church's identity and agency underdeveloped. For example, he considers the practice of discernment, rightly suggesting that "one of the most difficult challenges for Christians today is to test the spirits, to read the signs of the times, to see clearly where the line of division between the Kingdom and the antikingdom is today."[36] Yet, it is not always clear that it is the Church that is practicing such discernment. When he asks the question, "How do we discern the signs of the kingdom," he argues that the Kingdom of God can be located

---

32. Arias, *Announcing the Reign*, 53.

33. Arias, *Announcing the Reign*, 89. Arias quotes Carl Braaten, who writes, "Without its roots in the universal promise, missionary faith becomes indistinguishable from religious propaganda" (Braaten, *Flaming Center*, 54).

34. Arias, *Announcing the Reign*, 119-120.

35. Arias, *Announcing the Reign*, 119-120.

36. Arias, *Announcing the Reign*, 109.

where a just order is sought; there, where human life is respected and a full life is fostered; there, where women and men live in solidarity; there, where the structures of society try to favor "the orphan, the widow and the poor"; there, where human beings have the opportunity to become what God intends them to be; THERE, the kingdom of God is at work.[37]

While Arias persuasively illustrates what the Reign of God looks like, he is less clear when considering how the Church learns to see it. While framing evangelism in eschatological terms that lead him to acknowledge the theological necessity of the difference of Church/World, Arias is not always clear about the identity and agency of the Church, or about the necessity of such reflection in the construction of evangelistic mission.

We can find a clearer emphasis on the Church's place in a theology of evangelism in Abraham's work. Continuing emphasis on rooting evangelism inside a theological, eschatological frame, Abraham clarifies the various "agents" involved in the practice of evangelism.[38] In a section concerning the significance of the Holy Spirit to the practice of formation and particularly Confirmation, Abraham reminds us that the Holy Spirit's coming to the early Church was "a constitutive part of the fulfillment of the eschatological promises to Israel," thus clarifying the significance of the ecclesial community as the Body sent in mission.[39] At the same time, Abraham also reminds us that a commitment to the work of the Spirit clarifies that the Kingdom of God is not established by human means, but is the work of God to which the Church is sent into the world to witness. Here we find some mention of the challenge Christians face when sent into the world in evangelism: "Those called to give themselves in active service in the rule of God need some assurance that they do not face the world on their own but that they can face it with hope, knowing that they will be accompanied, led, and used by the Holy Spirit."[40] In this light, Abraham is led to reiterate the importance of initiation and formation for this engagement. Engaging the world in evangelistic mission "requires a life of watchfulness and discipline. It cannot be achieved without continuous recourse to the fountains of mercy, love, and grace provided in the church."[41] He goes

---

37. Arias, *Announcing the Reign*, 109.

38. Abraham, *Logic of Evangelism*, 103–4.

39. Abraham, *Logic of Evangelism*, 159.

40. Abraham, *Logic of Evangelism*, 159.

41. Abraham, *Logic of Evangelism*, 160.

on to clarify the necessity of spiritual disciplines, especially attendance at Eucharist, for such formation.[42]

With this clarification, it comes as no surprise that Abraham argues that the Church be considered one of four "agents" in evangelism, along with the Triune God, the evangelizer, and the evangelized.[43] Specifically addressing the role of the Church in evangelism, Abraham states that this community "is called to embody the rule of God in its worship, life, and ministries, to identify and to nourish those whom God has specially called to the work of evangelism, and to share with them in their characteristic activity as evangelists."[44] He strengthens these claims for the crucial mediating role of the Church in a theology of evangelism in an article written more than a decade later, where he says,

> While formally it is right to insist on a logical distinction between the church and the kingdom, contingently and in reality, there is no kingdom without a community, the church, and there is no church without the presence of the kingdom. God's reign has always had an Israel, an ecclesia, in history; it is not some sort of ahistorical, asocial reality.[45]

This density given the Church by Abraham in his later article then leads to his redeployment of the Church as a crucial agent in the practice of evangelism. Again, Abraham:

> to treat the church as just one dimension of entry into the kingdom is to underplay the place of the church in the work of making disciples. The life of the church is not just prudentially related to Christian discipleship; it is the place where one learns the very art of discipleship. . . . It is the church which has been commissioned by God to proclaim the gospel of the kingdom to all the world, to call all people into discipleship, and to provide the crucial teachings and practices which are the marks of all true disciples of Jesus

---

42. Abraham, *Logic of Evangelism*, 160–61.

43. Abraham, *Logic of Evangelism*, 103–4.

44. Abraham, *Logic of Evangelism*, 103.

45. In his chapter "On Making Disciples of the Lord Jesus Christ," Abraham argues that evangelism as initiation does not require "a choice between the church and the kingdom," but rather "a position which holds that both of these must be taken into consideration at once," and "when we do so we find that they complement each other in a deep way" (Abraham, "On Making Disciples," 159).

Christ. In short, it is the church which carries the right to identify the normative content of Christian initiation.[46]

This emphasis on the practices of formation help us to see the shape of the Church's agency in the practice of evangelism. In contrast to the somewhat understated account of the identity and agency of the Church we saw in Arias's work, Abraham makes a clear argument for ecclesial mediation in evangelism. Here the Church has priority, epistemically and practically and, in turn, this shapes the Church's evangelistic engagement with the world that it must pursue.

But it is at this point that Abraham's account leaves room for further development. He clearly acknowledges that an eschatological lens leads to a different way of seeing the world: "The world of eschatology is not our world; it is a strange universe of divine intervention and angelic activity, of Messiah and Son of Man, of woes and resurrections, of cosmic powers of evil, of vindications and judgments, of the end of time and history."[47] Further, Abraham is quite right to point out that to see the world in just this way is to assume a belief in a God who "created the world for certain intentions and purposes," and who remains active "in history and at the end of all history," seeking to fulfill these divine ends not through disembodied action, but rather through "the life of the people of Israel" who "pave the way for the coming of the kingdom in the life of Jesus of Nazareth."[48] In this context, Abraham's strong sense of the Church's identity and agency in the practice of evangelism is understandable and necessary if the Church is to engage faithfully with the "cosmic powers of evil" that constitute the world.

If this is the case, then why does Abraham not identify the world as one of the four "agents" in the practice of evangelism?[49] While it is possible that such an interpretation is assumed in his reference to the role played by the "unevangelized," this seems an unlikely reading, inasmuch as the Church and the "evangelist" are named separately.[50] Lacking the status of an agent in the framework, the account of the world Abraham offers lacks the texture we find in Arias's text. Abraham develops a description of the world engaging modernity, characterized by a creeping secularism in the modern

46. Abraham, "On Making Disciples," 160.

47. Abraham, *Logic of Evangelism*, 18.

48. Abraham, *Logic of Evangelism*, 20.

49. Once again, Abraham suggests these "agents" to be the Triune God, the Church, the evangelizer, and the evangelized. Abraham, *Logic of Evangelism*, 103–4.

50. Abraham, *Logic of Evangelism*, 103–4.

West, which has led to an evangelism shaped by technical and pragmatic concerns.[51] Alternatively, Abraham suggests a renewed Christian apologetics. Founded on the "internal logic of the Christian gospel," and if that engagement is grounded in "fortitude, patience, modesty, and a deep faith in the Holy Spirit," then there will be a way for Christians to engage "the modern world in all its shapes and forms with integrity and equanimity."[52] But the shape of this engagement, framed in the context of apologetics, has the effect of thinning out the identity and agency of the world being engaged.

What is required is a theology of evangelism that acknowledges the important but differentiated identities and roles played by both the Church and the world. But as we have seen, such an account is elusive. Now we turn to see that the development of such an account is also risky, just to the extent that it is subject to potential distortions. More particularly, we will see that the Church/World relationship inside theologies of evangelism tend to either "understate" or "overstate" the differentiated agencies of each. We seek a path between these polarities that we might see evangelism at the intersection of Church and world, leaning both ways at once.

Understating Church/World

The tendency to "understate" the distinction of Church and world develops from theological neglect of the differentiated identities and agencies associated with and ascribed to each. The lack of an adequate consideration of both almost certainly leads to the inevitable understatement of the differentiation and a tacit collapsing of one into the other: Church becomes synonymous with world. I believe a key example of this tendency at work in conversations related to the practice of evangelism can be found in the work of the Church Growth movement.

The twentieth-century reality of North American mainline congregational membership decline led to increased interest in evangelism focused on the goal of "church growth." In the frame of Church Growth, evangelism narrated a number of strategies and tactics a congregation might utilize to engage with its unbelieving environment, resulting in the

51. Abraham, *Logic of Evangelism*, 103–4. Abraham writes, "Modern evangelism has become a kind of entrepreneurial industry organized, funded, and run like a modern corporation" (Abraham, *Logic of Evangelism*, 200).

52. Abraham, *Logic of Evangelism*, 204, 205–6.

visible, measurable result of increasing worship attendance or (numerical) membership growth. Borrowing from missiological considerations of gospel contextualization and inculturation, Church Growth advocated for practices of translation and adaptation to increase the intelligibility and attraction of the gospel and ecclesial practices for a secular or "unchurched" population.

While concern for church growth helpfully pressed congregations to engage with communities outside the walls of the Church, I argue that it often did so without adequate theological consideration of the identity and the agency of the Church and, even more particularly, the world. This lack of attention to the theological leads to the "understatement" of the differentiation of Church/World, risking the collapse of one into the other and, ironically, weakening evangelistic witness.

One of the most significant Methodist voices in articulating a theology of evangelism governed by the goal of church growth is that of George G. Hunter III. Writing about Hunter, Paul Chilcote suggests that "few Methodists have published more in the area of evangelism. . . . Nearly all of Hunter's books touch on evangelism and Church growth in one way or another."[53] Such a focus leads Hunter to suggestions for the Church's adaptation of its message and practices, "attending to and adapting the lived gospel in dynamic ways to historical and cultural contexts."[54] Much of this stress has drawn Hunter's focus to issues of communication in evangelism, particularly the ways in which such communication might embolden the sharing of the Christian faith with a world less and less predisposed to or interested in such "good news." Hunter asks,

> How do you communicate the Christian faith to the growing numbers of "secular" people in the western world? . . . How do you communicate Christianity's meaning to people who do not darken church doors, who have no church background, who possess no traditional Christian vocabulary, who do not know what we are talking about? The question presses us with greater intensity as we realize that the countries and populations of the western world have become "mission fields" once again. . . . I have been obsessed with this question for over 25 years.[55]

---

53. Chilcote, "Evangelism in the Methodist Tradition," 234.

54. Chilcote, "Evangelism in the Methodist Tradition," 234.

55. Hunter, *How to Reach Secular People*, 13.

Pursuing this question, Hunter argues that each congregation must make the decision between (so-called) contrary ends, pursuing either "tradition" or "mission."[56] The former refers to the practices of the congregation that may have served the evangelistic outreach in prior generations and in other contexts, but that fail to do so in the here and now. The congregation's rigid adherence to this form of "tradition" curtails its capacity—its "mission"—to be engaged with and attractive to those on the outside, the unchurched. The choice of "mission" over "tradition" leads Churches to shape their practices in ways that facilitate outreach and evangelism to reach unchurched populations. Thus, Hunter argues that the problem with the "traditional" congregation is that people outside of the Church cannot but see it as culturally irrelevant. Here, evangelism is hindered from the start, because as "the church's members intuitively know that their unchurched friends cannot relate to [for example] Old East Side's style, language, liturgy, and music . . . they do not even consider inviting them."[57]

What then should the Church do? Hunter suggests a strategy: he calls the Church to communicate the Christian faith in ways that are "culturally appropriate" to the over "150 million secular people in the American mission field."[58] For the Church to pursue faithful and effective evangelistic mission in a given ministry context, the Church must seek to "adapt to the language and culture of the people we are called to reach," which constitutes an "indigenous" strategy for ministry.[59] Hunter continues,

> At the surface level, an indigenous ministry strategy involves adapting to the style, the language, the aesthetics, and the music of the target population. (SLAM serves as a convenient acronym.) At a deeper level, indigenous ministry involves engaging the attitudes, beliefs, and values characteristic of the society, especially the core attitudes, beliefs, and values that provide the lens, or the "worldview" through which the society views the world.[60]

When turned toward the congregation, this lens provides the interpretive frame through which the "traditions" of the congregation, its programs and practices, can be adapted for the sake of evangelistic mission.

56. Hunter, *Radical Outreach*, 18.
57. Hunter, *Radical Outreach*, 73.
58. Hunter, *Radical Outreach*, 75.
59. Hunter, *Radical Outreach*, 33.
60. Hunter, *Radical Outreach*, 33.

Hunter is quite right about the need for the Church to engage the world in evangelistic mission (indeed, this is the point at the center of this book's concern!). Too many congregations have neglected the calling to be engaged "beyond the walls," and Hunter's work, alongside so many others in conversations about the "missional church," stands as a crucial contribution to the possibility of the Church's evangelistic witness in the twenty-first century.[61] Hunter is also right to point to the nature of the congregation's engagement with its context embodied in a concern for the contextualization or inculturation of the Church's witness. The translation of the gospel is not an optional practice in the missional identity of the Church, given the diversity of contexts where the Church is embodied. I fear, however, that pressing evangelistic mission in the way he does, Hunter inadvertently posits underdeveloped accounts of both the Church and the world in which it serves.

First, given the focus on congregational growth, the Church is primarily identified in the programs and practices that either do aim at the goal of evangelistic outreach ("mission") or that do not ("tradition"). This leaves unclear whether the Church has an identity beyond its role as a location or perhaps as a "container" for the activities that proclaim the gospel and form Christian discipleship. Framed as such, it is difficult to see a sense of identity or agency given the Church beyond its instrumental purpose, housing the outreaching activities deployed in the evangelistic task. Of course, the Church *is* sometimes rightly identified as an instrument (often alongside the descriptions of the Church also as "sign" and "foretaste") of the Kingdom of God. The question raised here is not whether a focus on the Church as instrument is wrong, but rather, whether this focus on Church growth draws *too much* focus to this instrumental identity. Is Church best understood as the organizational collection, the container of missional and formational Christian practices shaped to be in service to evangelistic ends? While the Church is an instrument, is it not also more than an instrument?

To ask the question in a slightly different way, we could wonder what it means to say that the Church is "holy" (alongside its calling to be apostolic, one, and catholic, per the creedal affirmation). The difference that holiness makes in the identity and agency of the Church is to pose an ecclesiological question that is, here, mostly unasked and unanswered. In turn, what

61. For a helpful historical account of the background and diverse developments of the term "missional," see Van Gelder and Zscheile, *Missional Church in Perspective*.

is understated here is an account of the Church's identity and agency in evangelistic mission.

Second, this focus on church growth also tends to neglect a fully developed account of the identity and agency of the world. In much the same way the Church is rendered as a container of programs and practices meant to be adapted and utilized in evangelistic mission, the world also is pictured here as a container of linguistic and aesthetic cultures readily available to shape the adaptation of ecclesial practices. Again, while the contextualization of the Church and the translation of the Gospel are inevitable realities, the question posed here is whether concerns for church growth have adequately assessed what is at stake when borrowing from or adapting to its context.

Thus we might ask whether the work of congregations to develop multiple programmatic offerings shaped to serve increasingly segmented niche populations is an example of responsive and effective evangelism or a surrender to the necessity of congregational competition in an ecclesial market economy full of "church shoppers."[62] Is such use to be understood as practicing "indigenous" adaptations in the Christian practices of worship that lead to greater perceived cultural relevance and subsequently, a more effective evangelistic outreach, or is the Church simply submitting to the service of greater powers in the world? While answering such questions would take us beyond our purpose here (and will receive more attention in chapter 2), it is enough to suggest that it is a larger problem not to ask such questions at all. In other words, when the Church does not ask how far it might lean into the world without falling in, the Church enters the world at the greatest risk of taking such a fall. This is the danger of the understatement of the differentiation of Church and world.

Overstating Church/World

While the difference holiness makes can be understated, risking the collapse of the Church into the world, it is equally problematic to overstate the difference, risking the separation of the Church from the world. It may seem strange to suggest that anyone concerned with evangelism might introduce or endorse distance between the congregation and its context, but as a reaction to the understatement described above, the focus can shift from concern for the effectiveness of the Church's outreach seeking

62. Kenneson, "Selling [Out] the Church."

congregational growth to concern for maintaining the integrity of the Church's faithful identity. If the work of Hunter considered above stands as a key example of the tendency to understate the Church/World distinction, I turn next to consider Bryan Stone's work in *Evangelism after Christendom* as an example of the alternative.[63]

Echoing Outler's concerns over limited understandings of evangelism in the post-Great Awakening period, Stone agrees that modern Protestantism has seen the minimization of evangelism to personal "decision" or "experience," reflecting the individualizing forces of modernity and an overdeveloped focus on justification as the entrance into Christian faith (ignoring the importance of sanctification). Thus, Stone also decries the focus of evangelism in modernity as one that introduces the evangelized to particular Christian beliefs rather than to the activities and practices that form and shape one's life into something Christlike. In other words, Stone will agree that a focus on the relationship of initiation and discipleship to evangelism is crucial. However, unlike other writers in the Methodist tradition, Stone roots this problem in the collapse of the theological distinction of Church/World. Stone writes:

> As their foundation, the ethical, soteriological, and eschatological distortions of evangelism come as consequences of its being narrated by a Constantinian account of history and of the loss of a proper distinction between church and world, with a resulting loss of distinctive witness by the church in the world.[64]

Opposed to Hunter, who seeks a relevant evangelism guiding the shape of the Church's identity and practices (making the Church more familiar and less distinct), Stone seeks to root a theology of evangelism in "the actual lived habits of the very Church which invites the world around to consider its habituated gospel."[65] In short, Stone places focus on the identity and agency of the Church as central to an account of evangelism construed as witness to a watching world.

The focus on reading history with "non-Constantinian" eyes and on the necessity of a theological Church/World distinction reveals Stone's Hauerwasian understanding of the Church's practices of formation and witness. "The thesis of this book," Stone writes, paraphrasing Hauerwas, "is that the most evangelistic thing the church can do today is to be the

63. Stone, *Evangelism after Christendom*.

64. Stone, *Evangelism after Christendom*, 126–27.

65. Chilcote, "Evangelism in the Methodist Tradition," 236.

church."[66] For Stone, this activity is "to be formed imaginatively by the Holy Spirit through core practices such as worship, forgiveness, hospitality, and economic sharing into a distinctive people in the world, a new social option, the body of Christ."[67] From this ecclesiological beginning, Stone develops a theology of evangelism that rejects the apologetic mode (on display in Hunter's work) and replaces it with a strong focus on the formative community of the witnessing Church, shaped to witness to a distinctive way of life in the world.

However, this is not to argue, as we see in Hunter's work, that the North American Church is best understood as the storehouse of practices instrumentally effective for Christian mission. Rather, Stone says, "it is only by being drawn into communion that individuals become 'persons' in the first place and thereby transcend the modern constitution of the self as individualized being. Hauerwas is exactly right, therefore, when he says, 'The first words about the Christian life are about a life together, not about the individual.'"[68] Consequently, this communal focus also takes the focus away from the necessity of the Church's growth through individual conversions as a sign of successful evangelism. Stone makes this quite clear when he writes:

> It is important . . . to state and argue for the following premise as clearly and straightforwardly as possible as to avoid any misunderstanding: while evangelism seeks to draw persons into the life of the church as a way of inviting them to a journey of conversion, the quantitative growth of the church *is no positive indication whatsoever* that God's intention of creating a new people is being fulfilled or that God's reign is breaking into history.[69]

A central concern for community in Stone's work gives the Church (rather than individual Christians) a primary agency in the practice of evangelism.

In a sense, Stone's book is an effort to define the shape of ecclesial agency in evangelism, described in the subtitle as the practice of "Christian Witness." As evangelism is a practice "performed at boundaries and along the edges of difference," presumably between Church/World, then "nothing could be more important to a theology of evangelism," Stone argues, "than

66. Stone, *Evangelism after Christendom*, 15.

67. Stone, *Evangelism after Christendom*, 15.

68. Stone, *Evangelism after Christendom*, 262.

69. Stone, *Evangelism after Christendom*, 271.

clarifying the nature of that difference and how the Christian community's posture toward the world along those boundaries is always one of both invitation and subversion."[70] Stone clarifies that this difference is always shaped by the object of the Church's witness: Jesus. Thus, Stone argues that because evangelism is shaped by the life, death, and resurrection of Jesus, "we may affirm that the politics of evangelism is, from beginning to end, pacifist."[71] In other words, evangelism is concerned not with strategies and tactics that seek to guarantee the consent and conversion of the unbelieving, so-called "unchurched." To be so preoccupied would be to give in to a sort of epistemic violence and to replace faithful witness with the pursuit of economic ends embodied in the need to secure outcomes measured by numerical growth in the Church. Instead, guided by the confession that Jesus is Lord, the Church cannot help but to live an evangelistic life of witness, only requiring "the peaceable simplicity of an offer and an invitation to 'come and see' (John 1:46)."[72]

But this is where we must press further to get at Stone's sense of that agency. What is the shape of that offer and invitation? What practices constitute such witness? Stone is quick to clarify that this stance does not exonerate the Church from a calling to engage in a form of apologetics when relating to the world, inasmuch as the "character of Christian evangelism is not only invitation but also summons."[73] However, in order to keep faith with the peaceable Lord proclaimed, a pacifist evangelism engages apologetics not on epistemological or metaphysical terms, but rather, Stone argues, on "aesthetic" terms.[74] To rely on any other foundation would be to supplant Jesus as the foundation for the Church's apologetic witness, and so, eschewing that, "evangelism relies from first to last on the beauty of holiness made real in the church by the operation of the Holy Spirit."[75] This certainly means that the visibility of the Church and its practices in the world are key to the agency the Church has in evangelistic witness. So framed, the Church's evangelism is subversive just to the extent that it offers visible, embodied practices that stand apart from the ways of the world and

---

70. Stone, *Evangelism after Christendom*, 172.
71. Stone, *Evangelism after Christendom*, 229.
72. Stone, *Evangelism after Christendom*, 12.
73. Stone, *Evangelism after Christendom*, 12.
74. Stone, *Evangelism after Christendom*, 267–68.
75. Stone, *Evangelism after Christendom*, 267–68.

that model a peaceable way of life in the way of Jesus.[76] At the same time, these practices are forms of invitational evangelism, just to the extent that they provide a means for the world to see these alternative ways of life "in action." Stone writes that "the visibility of [Christians'] witness affords us clues to how we might better share the beauty of holiness, which is the 'apologetic' link between faithful witness and the imaginative, alluring, and captivating reception of that witness in the world."[77] In other words, Stone argues for the Church's agency in witness to be understood in primarily "aesthetic" terms.[78]

This stance becomes even more understandable against the backdrop of Stone's understanding of the identity and agency of the world, under-stood explicitly as the created, yet fallen realm of disobedient principalities and powers. In these terms, contra Hunter, the world is not a neutral terri-tory from which the Church can unreflectively borrow, nor is the world a market to which the Church must be made relevant. Rather, in relationship to this world, the Church must engage in an evangelism that is in, but not of, the world. For Stone, this requires not only the rejection of Hunter's understatement of the Church/World difference, but a reassertion of that difference. At the same time, it is a careful position of the Church in rela-tionship to that world. Because there is so much at stake in this engagement with the world, the Church does not seek strategies for relevance or other tactical engagements as much as it simply offers the consistency and beauty of its own life in holiness, the Church being the Church. This is evangelism as aesthetics.

While Stone takes Church/World seriously, locating the Church's evangelistic witness in the aesthetic display of its beautiful life to a so-called watching world, I am concerned with the move to locate that agency pri-marily, if not entirely, in aesthetic terms. To limit the evangelistic engage-ment of the Church and the world to terms of "invitation" and "subversion" as Stone seems to do is to leave too much unsaid about the nature of their intersection. In this way, while Stone represents an alternative to Hunter's understatement, I want to lodge the concern that he creates the conditions

76. Stone writes, "Evangelism will have to be understood . . . as a fundamentally sub-versive activity, born out of a posture of eccentricity (living 'off center' or 'outside the center,' at the margins) and out of the cultivation of such deviant practices as sharing bread with the poor, loving enemies, refusing violence, forgiving sins, and telling the truth" (Stone, *Evangelism after Christendom*, 13).

77. Stone, *Evangelism after Christendom*, 278.

78. Stone, *Evangelism after Christendom*, 230–38.

for an overcorrection, resulting in a position that *overstates* the difference of Church/World in evangelism. In short, I want Stone to say more about the shape of that intersection between agents in evangelism and to move toward a position that leans both ways at once.

Stone's formation of a set of conditions conducive to Church/World overstatement begins with his identification of the Church as "the primary cultural and linguistic context for evangelism and conversion."[79] This is an uncontroversial claim until it is paired with his concern for articulating the Church's engagement with the world in evangelism. This leads Stone to consider "the initial process of invitation and formation" which "begins with an imaginative 'drawing' of persons into a new world by the church that . . . if apologetic at all, is so in a chiefly aesthetic sense."[80] While such a position charts a course that seeks to keep the church from losing itself in the evangelistic engagement with the world, the question raised here is whether it says too little about what sorts of engagements are possible beyond the appeal to an "aesthetic" apologetic.

Stone does point out that evangelistic outreach allows for a further particularization and contextualization of the Church's practices for the purpose of faithfully presenting the gospel through the Church exactly where it is and with whom it lives. However, I believe that Stone lacks a substantive consideration and exemplary illustration of how this particular practice literally "works" in a congregational context. While Stone emphasizes evangelism by virtue of the Church's aesthetic offering of its own life, that life surely does include forms of engagement with the world. For instance, we can point to examples of such engagement in the Church's participation in processes of forgiveness and reconciliation and in the development of health care and educational institutions. Stone knows this, but in his account of evangelism, he leaves this acknowledgment understated, so that the reader is left with the conclusion that the purity and the holiness of the Church's internal life is the primary source for its evangelistic witness.

We can find a similar dynamic in Samuel Wells's consideration of evangelism in his book, *God's Companions: Reimagining Christian Ethics.*[81] Wells's study "locates the heart of ethics squarely in the practices of the local Church," considering the intersection of the Church's ethical action and

---

79. Stone, *Evangelism after Christendom*, 267.

80. Stone, *Evangelism after Christendom*, 267–68.

81. Wells, *God's Companions.*

its formation, particularly in worship.[82] Some of this action in the world is evangelism. For Wells, "Evangelism names a variety of practices by which the Church invites all people to worship God, to be his friends, and to eat with him."[83] However, he is careful not to equate "conversion" with "evangelism," understanding that evangelism is that mode of invitation that brings one into the orbit of the Church. Conversion comes later through forms of catechesis, including regular participation in worship and presumably other practices of the Church's shared life that eventually lead to Baptism, one's formal entrance into the Church. Drawn narrowly then, the elements that comprise evangelism for Wells include "all those conversations, events, communications, gestures, encounters through which a person comes to hear and receive that invitation made by God through the Church."[84] While such a general statement would invite a request for further clarification, Wells does not stop with this identification, and goes further to argue that these forms of evangelistic mission take two forms, "prophetic" and "priestly," while avoiding a third, that being "kingly," evangelism. Each of these treatments deserves some brief attention.

Wells argues that "prophetic evangelism" refers to all those activities "whose principal or entire purpose is to bring people face to face with God, especially when such people have forgotten or never known what it means to worship [God], to be [God's] friends, and eat with [God]."[85] The primary way in which this takes place, according to Wells, is through the Church's work of witness, understood to be a subtle, yet constant and visible presence of the Church in the world that is eventually noticed by the world exactly because of its presence and constancy. A further extension of this prophetic mode is found beyond evangelism as prophetic "witness" when it becomes prophetic "martyrdom." While these terms are synonymous, Wells believes that it is helpful to suggest the role of martyr as an escalation of Christian witness-as-presence that more directly challenges the very order of things in the world, and thus, suggests a different and riskier set of consequences for the Christian evangelist; whereas evangelism in the mode of witness may result in inviting the world's ridicule, evangelism as martyr may invite the world's wrath.[86]

82. Wells, God's Companions, 5.

83. Wells, God's Companions, 57.

84. Wells, God's Companions, 57–58.

85. Wells, God's Companions, 58.

86. Wells, God's Companions, 60.

Prophetic evangelism is therefore different from Wells's second type, "Priestly Evangelism." Turning toward the witness of the internal life of the Church, priestly evangelism refers to "activity that falls appropriately within the common life of the Church, and is conducted for its own sake, but through which the grace of God may nonetheless touch a person and inspire them to discover more of the hope that is in the hearts of Christians."[87] In other words, if one is exposed to the inherent beauty found in the lives of Christians and in the shared life of the Christian community and comes to see it as both attractive and habitable, then perhaps this too can be a persuasive form of witness as one responds with the decision to enter the Catechumenate. This witness is not to be limited to the interior life of the Church, however, and so Wells offers a second mode of priestly evangelism understood as "humble" involvement outside the Church in the local community, the Church essentially being the Church in the neighborhood where it has been placed. While prophetic evangelism is an inherent challenge to the way of the world, priestly evangelism is a mode of the Church's grace-full presence in the world.[88]

Neither type of evangelism engages in an apologetic task of adapting the gospel or the Church's practices to forms more familiar or relevant to the world. Such a strategy constitutes a key example of Wells's third type of evangelism, taking on the "kingly" stance. Here, the Church takes the ends of evangelism into its own hands, controlling the shape of witness in order to exercise some control over the results. As Wells puts it, kingly evangelism "directs attention away from Christ" and toward the Church, and in this way, subverts the possibility of faithful witness.[89] As we have seen, while neglect of this issue leads some to push the Church into the world without any critical consideration of the mode of the Church's presence in the world, Wells counsels restraint, seeking a way for the Church to be evangelistically present in the world without suffering the loss of its own identity in the process. Priestly and prophetic evangelism emerge out of the primary practices of the Church being the Church, through the life of a community that is a witness in the world.[90] As Wells sums it up, "In short, the Church is a prophet and priest that points to a king."[91]

87. Wells, *God's Companions*, 58.

88. Wells, *God's Companions*, 61–62.

89. Wells, *God's Companions*, 62.

90. Wells, *God's Companions*, 62.

91. Wells, *God's Companions*, 62.

Wells's work reflects care for the differentiation of Church and world and holds a significant place for intra-ecclesial ministry in an account of evangelistic mission. Yet, could it be that this position may actually function to undermine that evangelistic mission, just to the extent that his account may overstate the difference of the Church and the world? Once again, the issue here is the possibility that the Church's missional relationship to the world is primarily identified with, or perhaps even limited to, the aesthetic witness of an alternative community that offers itself as an "example" or a "display" of holiness.

But in the resistance to the kingly mode, is the Church pursuing an evangelistic mission that is denied the agency necessary for a strong account of the Church's engagement with the world? For instance, Hunter might ask Wells for a closer account of the forms of evangelistic practice he names as "all those conversations, events, communications, gestures, encounters through which a person comes to hear and receive that invitation made by God through the Church."[92] Focused as he has been on issues of communication, Hunter's concern will be for Wells to display an adequate understanding of interpersonal conversation that shows cultural competency and thus, a more effective evangelistic effort.

Whether or not one agrees with Hunter's own construction of evangelistic practice, the challenge he represents is important. Stone and Wells both helpfully emphasize the primary role of the Church in evangelism, effectively drawing the Church back from its often-unquestioned, apologetic lean into the world associated with the understated differentiation of Church/World. But does it go too far, potentially overcorrecting this problem? If Christian witness is primarily associated with or limited to the aesthetic display of the Church's internal life of holiness, then this leaves room to develop a more robust, complicated account of the ways the Church engages the world in the practice of evangelism.

Conclusion

I have argued that a focus on the Church/World distinction is crucial to the formation of a faithful theology of evangelistic mission. I have also suggested that the balance between Church and world has been difficult to maintain, as we have seen how the relationship and distinction of Church/World can fall out of balance, tending either toward understatement or overstatement.

92. Wells, *God's Companions*, 57–58.

To move beyond these limitations, we will turn next to consider more carefully the differentiated identities and agencies associated with the Church and the world. Considering both will prelude the constructive task in later chapters, namely, articulating a Methodist ecclesiology and theology of evangelism that leans both ways at once.

2

The World

What are principalities and powers? What is their significance in
the creation and in the fall? What is their relationship to human
sin? How are these powers related to the presence and power of
death in history? What is the meaning of the confrontation between Christ and the principalities? Does a Christian have any
freedom from their dominion? There can be no serious, realistic,
or biblical comprehension of the witness of the Church in the
world unless such questions as these are raised and pondered.[1]

Introduction

ON THE WAY TOWARD developing a Methodist theology of evangelism that
takes seriously the Church/World distinction, avoiding problematic over-
and understatement, we begin with consideration of the identity and the
agency of the world. When the Church engages in evangelistic mission, it
must acknowledge the complexity within which all such action occurs. The
Church's life and its practice of evangelism all take place in time, in history,
or—in biblical terms—within the "world." This is not to say that when we
speak of the world we speak of a neutral "context" or an inert "environment" within which evangelists choose freely how to engage in the proclamation of the gospel. More specifically, to speak of the world is to speak of
Creation, at once called good by the God who formed it and yet fallen and

---

1. Stringfellow, *Free in Obedience*, 51–52.

under the sway of disobedient principalities and powers. While language concerning "the powers" has played an increasingly significant role within twentieth-century theology and ethics (after a long period of absence in theological discourse), it has not played as significant a role in contemporary practical theology, save for a few counter-examples.[2] However, in the larger effort to articulate a theology and practice of evangelism within the distinction of Church and world, these reflections are required. They are required precisely because to see an environment as creation, or as the "world" of principalities and powers, is a theological judgment, and to determine the shape of the Church's evangelistic engagement with that world requires theological judgment. Thus, some account of formation is necessary to shape such judgment.

The relationship of evangelism and formation is a key issue derivative of the larger concern for the relationship of the Church and the world. In short, a concern for formation without evangelism pushes the Church toward sectarianism (described in the prior chapter as overstatement of the Church/World distinction), and an account of mission without formation pushes the Church toward unquestioning, apologetic translation (previously described as understatement). Concern for both formation and mission is a "leaning both ways" in the life of the Church that nurtures both fidelity to tradition and authentic engagement in context. A consideration of the theological status of the world is necessary to develop this point, in order to prepare the way for the development of a missional ecclesiology that seeks to lean both ways at once, always into both formation and evangelism. Thus, in this chapter, I ask, what is the agency of the world, and what is its impact on a theology of evangelism?

To ask such questions, however, is to invite the skepticism of contemporary Methodists. After all, it was none other than John Wesley himself who said, "I look upon all the world as my parish,"[3] and contemporary United Methodists claim their mission to "make disciples of Jesus Christ

2. Marva Dawn offers a brief summary of this history in chapter 1 of her book, *Powers, Weakness, and the Tabernacling of God*. However, hers is just one of a very few works that explicitly reflects upon the principalities and powers in entering into conversation with contemporary forms of practical theology. See also Campbell, *Word Before the Powers*.

3. This is a quotation often taken out of context. Addressing the concerns of those critical of his unconventional decision to engage in field preaching regardless of parish boundaries, Wesley said, "I look upon all the world as my parish; thus far, I mean, that in whatever part of it I am I judge it meet, right, and my bounden duty to declare, unto all that are willing to hear, the glad tidings of salvation" (Wesley, *Letters*, 1:286).

for the transformation of the world."[4] Yet, to begin the chapter's argument, I will show the ways in which many contemporary Methodist theologies tend to emphasize the created goodness of the world without adequate attention paid to the world as also fallen, a balance that we find in Wesley's own theological vision. Wesley argued for formation in holiness that defined the Methodist movement and that nurtured a "People called Methodist" who exercised care for their relationship with the world. But such commitment dissipated over time, embodied in an unmediated, unquestioned engagement of Methodists with the unbelieving world. For Wesley, a focus on the identity and agency of the world as well as on the crucial practices of formation in holiness constituted a way of being in the world that leaned both ways at once. While clearly called to the mission of spreading scriptural holiness, Methodists risked losing themselves in the engagement when not simultaneously attending to their need for formation and to the agency of principalities and powers.

Having lost this balance, contemporary Methodists tend to frame evangelistic mission according to the belief that the particularities of culture and practice within each context represent not a challenge or threat, but rather, a set of materials useable in the formation of the Church's witness. Relatedly, we find an understated emphasis on the significance of formation in relationship to accounts of evangelism. Turning to Wesley and his tradition on the subject of the world, we will rediscover the need for a further engagement with the identity and agency of the principalities and powers for the development of evangelistic theology and practice. Without a robust account of the agency of the world as well as an account of the significance of formation, Methodist theologies of evangelism will fail to keep a balance that leans both ways at once.

Addressing this lack in contemporary Methodist theology, I turn next to a deeper articulation of the identity and agency of the principalities and powers of the fallen world. We will see that the powers of the world are both created yet fallen. In this fallen state, they function with a self-serving agency located in the formation of imagination, perception, and desire. To clarify the context and content of this formation, I will connect these reflections on the world to the work of David Yeago and Vincent Miller, who will help us to identify the market in late-modern North American life as a primary instantiation of the powers and principalities, and as a

4. United Methodist Church, *Book of Discipline 2016*, para. 120.

key example of their capacity to shape the imagination and inevitably, the ministry of the Church.

A properly Methodist theology of evangelism will seek a balanced vision of the world that understands the necessity and the danger of evangelistic mission within a creation that is simultaneously fallen, disobedient, and yet, created as good and yearning for redemptive fulfillment. Thus, I conclude with some reflections on the relationship between formation and evangelistic mission in recent Methodist evangelism and will suggest that without a robust account of the agency of the world within the Church/World distinction, theologies of evangelism will fail to keep a balance that leans both ways at once.

Wesleyan/Methodist Reflections on the World

Wesley established a balanced account of the world, acknowledging both its goodness as creation and the lingering effects of the fall. While we might say that Wesley's account leaned both ways at once, Methodist theological tradition after Wesley has struggled to retain such a balance. Here an overly positive vision of the world reigns, leaning only one way—rightly emphasizing the goodness of creation, but often at the expense of a truthful account of its fallenness.

From inside the Wesleyan and Methodist traditions, the status of the world may appear obvious: "I look upon the whole world as my parish," Wesley said.[5] As Dana Robert and Douglas Tzan note, this sentence is often deployed "as the quintessential statement of Methodism's identity as a mission movement," underwriting a wide variety of expressions, ranging from international missionary work, evangelistic outreach, and social service.[6] It is often conjured as a source that informs congregational mission in The United Methodist Church, called "to make disciples of Jesus Christ . . . for the transformation of the world."[7] As Robert and Tzan sum it up, "Born as a movement to reform the church and to spread 'scriptural holiness' across

---

5. Wesley, *Letters*, 1:286. To reiterate, as Robert and Tzan rightly note, in Wesley's original context, he wrote "these defiant words in response to being denied use of a pulpit on grounds that he violated church order. He consequently moved into the fields where he could reach those who lacked a church home" (Robert and Tzan, "Traditions and Transitions," 431).

6. Robert and Tzan, "Traditions and Transitions," 431.

7. United Methodist Church, *Book of Discipline 2016*, para. 120.

the land, the tradition of Methodism is to move outwards into the world with a message of free grace and social concern."[8] By these lights, the world has a relatively uncontroversial status: it is where Methodists are sent to teach, to serve, and to proclaim the gospel.

But the question we pursue here is not only one of missiology, but of theology: what is the theological identity and agency of the world for Methodists? From a theological perspective, the world is first and foremost the Creation, the good work of the Creator who spoke into being all that is and called it good. As Randy Maddox points out, John Wesley clearly shared this commitment, defended the doctrine of *creatio ex nihilo,* and affirmed that if God is the source of all, then creation must be endowed with an original goodness (prior, of course, to the introduction of sin).[9] Wesley also affirmed that the God who created is also the God who sustains the creation, the parent who offers an unfailing, providential order and loving care to all things.[10] In more Wesleyan terms, this providence is expressed as divine grace and is offered universally to the whole creation. This outlook had particular significance for Wesley's theological anthropology; as Maddox notes, "Wesley's most fundamental conviction about human life was that we are created dependent beings. Our very existence and all of our faculties are gifts of God's grace."[11]

While it is important to keep this commitment to the goodness of creation in sight, it is also the case that Wesley offered a rounded account of the fall and of the crucial doctrine of original sin. Again, as Maddox notes, Wesley "rarely passed up an opportunity to affirm the universal problem of human sinfulness. He considered any denial of this reality to be both contrary to general experience and a fundamental rejection of Christianity."[12] This sinfulness, however, was not just an issue located within his theological anthropology; indeed, not only humans, but all of creation has fallen. In humanity's disobedience to its Creator, Wesley posits effects not limited to the interiority of the human heart, but present throughout all creation. Wesley makes this clear in his sermon, "God's Approbation of His Works," noting that when humans oppose God, "a whole army of evils, totally new, totally unknown till then, broke in upon rebel man, and all other creatures,

---

8. Robert and Tzan, "Traditions and Transitions," 433.

9. Maddox, *Responsible Grace,* 59.

10. Maddox, *Responsible Grace,* 60.

11. Maddox, *Responsible Grace,* 67.

12. Maddox, *Responsible Grace,* 73.

and overspread the face of the earth."[13] The echo of the fall sounds throughout the creation.

Yet, as Theodore Runyon rightly notes, for Wesley, "God does not
abandon this creature to the consequences of disobedience."[14] While Wesley's great concern was to articulate a *via salutis* that described the work of
grace in the justification and sanctification of human lives, it becomes evident, particularly in his later years, that Wesley also showed concern for the
redemption of all creation, human and non-human, from its fallen state.[15]
Rather than placing eschatological hope only in a heavenly world to come,
Wesley shifts his concern to the renewal of this material world. In turn,
this shift influences Wesley's understanding of the mission of the Church.
Yet, here we get ahead of ourselves. The aim here is to note a balance in
the Wesleyan theological perspective concerning the state of the world. In
short, the world is created, and thus, the world is good. At the same time,
just as the creation has fallen into sin, so too has the world, created but
fallen and waiting for its full redemption. With this balance in place, the
question can next be asked: how shall Methodists live faithfully *in* but not
of the world? The commitments entailed by confronting these questions
influenced Wesley's guidance for the People called Methodist.

In two sermons, both developed and published late in his life, Wesley
clearly and strongly asserted that Methodist Christians must seek some
separation from the world (clearly understood to be non-Christian people)
who would threaten their growing faith. In the first of these two sermons,
Wesley writes:

> There can be no profitable "fellowship" between the righteous and
> the unrighteous; as there can be no "communion" between light
> and darkness.... As Christ can have no "concord" with Belial, so a
> believer in him can have no concord with an unbeliever.[16]

---

13. Wesley, "God's Approbation," §2.3, *Works*, 2:399.

14. Runyon, *New Creation*, 11.

15. This shift is particularly evident in Wesley's later sermons, where, as Maddox
notes, Wesley expresses distinctly postmillennial eschatological commitments. Thus,
"his focus of redemptive expectation increasingly shifted from a transcendent Heaven
to a future New Creation," appearing in an "eschatological vision of spreading the Reign
of God in individual lives, social structures, and creation at large" (Maddox, *Responsible
Grace*, 240–42).

16. Wesley, "In What Sense," §8, *Works*, 3:146.

Wesley then clarifies why this is the case, describing the differentiation of Church and world behind this warning:

> They are subjects not only of two separate, but of two opposite kingdoms. They act upon quite different principles: they aim at different ends. It will necessarily follow that frequently, if not always, they will walk in different paths.[17]

What is remarkable about this assertion is not only Wesley's strong warning, but also the vision of the world upon which it is based, a vision that shows concern for the world (and for those within it) as both the creation of God and yet also corrupted in the fall.

Still, this delineation of the two Kingdoms and the stern warning he offers cannot be overstated; Wesley still believed that Methodists must engage the unbelieving other. In the later sermon, "On Friendship with the World," Wesley clarifies that those "of the world" are still deserving of Christian concern. He writes "we ought to love them as ourselves (for they also are included in the word 'neighbour')"—and thereby we can fulfill the basic requirement of the second greatest commandment.[18] In relationship to those who are in the world, Wesley preaches that Methodists are called "to bear them real goodwill; to desire their happiness as sincerely as we desire the happiness of our own souls."[19] This statement seems surprising. Given the stark description of the "two separate" and "opposite kingdoms" in the first sermon, why would Wesley encourage the Methodists to practice this kind of friendship with the world?

The answer is that Wesley continues to make room, even in a sermon warning Methodists about the dangers of the world, for an account of the world's created goodness. This is a goodness established in the original creative act, but not limited there, as the work of God in Christ is an expression of saving grace for all creation. He writes:

> Yea, we are in a sense to honour them [non-Christians who constitute the world] (seeing that we are directed by the Apostle to "honour all men") as the creatures of God; nay, as immortal spirits who are capable of knowing, of loving, and of enjoying him to all eternity. We are to honour them as redeemed by his blood who "tasted death for every man."[20]

17. Wesley, "In What Sense," §8, *Works*, 3:146.
18. Wesley, "On Friendship," §8, *Works*, 3:130.
19. Wesley, "On Friendship," §8, *Works*, 3:130.
20. Wesley, "On Friendship," §8, *Works*, 3:130–31.

Such theological commitments have ethical and specifically evange-listic ramifications. Methodists are called "to speak to them on all occasions in the most kind and obliging manner we can," and "to do to them all the good that is in our power, all they are willing to receive from us," as a means to follow the example "of the universal Friend, our Father which is in heaven."[21] Created by God, initially pardoned through the work of God in Christ, and empowered in the prevenient graceful work of the Holy Spirit, those who inhabit the unfaithful world are loved by God. Christian Methodists are called to echo that divine love for the world.

Still, as strong as Wesley's description of the goodness of the world may be in these sermons, his warnings about the world dominate, and this is because of Wesley's sense of the danger that those in the world pose to the sustenance of Methodist faith and life. While Wesley holds the created goodness of the world in one hand, he clearly holds the doctrine of original sin and creation's fall in the other. But what is significant about Wesley's treatment of this issue is the nuanced way in which he conceives of the danger the world poses. He understands that Christian friendship with the world will not "immediately lead us into any outward sin."[22] Wesley's concern is not with the changes this friendship will render in discrete acts or overt choices, but rather, he draws attention to the more subtle ways a Christian perspective will suffer. More specifically, within Wesley's understanding of human moral development, what others call his "moral psychology," engagement with the world constitutes a counter-formation to the journey Christians make toward perfection. A brief consideration of the structure of his moral psychology will be required for us to understand fully Wesley's warning to Methodists concerning their engagement with the world.

As Randy Maddox argues, salvation for Wesley included more than just "deliverance from hell, or going to heaven."[23] Salvation for Wesley was "restoration of the soul" or "renewal" of the image of God in holiness, a condition that assumes the formation of holy tempers.[24] This assumption draws Wesley's moral psychology into the conversation. Wesley's "moral

21. Wesley, "On Friendship," §8, *Works*, 3:131.

22. Wesley, "In What Sense," §9, *Works*, 3:146.

23. Wesley, "Farther Appeal," §3, *Works*, 11:106; quoted by Maddox, "Wesley's Prescription," 18.

24. Wesley, "Farther Appeal," §3, *Works*, 11:106; quoted by Maddox, "Wesley's Prescription," 18.

psychology" articulated the role of the "affections" and "tempers" to inform an account of human moral action, as opposed to rival theories that emphasized the central importance of reason's capacity to subdue emotion for the development of right action.[25] Where the affections, for Wesley, addressed the "motivating dispositions," the tempers reflected the "enduring or *habitual* disposition of a person."[26] Taken together, "the capacity for affections is part of the Image of God" in the person, and "the proper enduring orientation of these affections would constitute the Christian tempers (or inward holiness) which is the Likeness of God."[27] However, because the corruption of sin affects the affections and tempers, salvation must address this need for renewal and re-formation. It does this via justifying and sanctifying grace, communicated in the instituted and prudential means through which believers are nurtured on their journey toward having "the mind of Christ." As Maddox puts it, "if present salvation is ultimately expressed in holy living, it is grounded in the transformation of our distorted unholy tempers into holy tempers."[28] The means of this formation are located in the Church, and even more particularly, for Maddox, in the practices of "social grace" therein.[29] This "social grace," however, cannot be solely located in the Church's practices as a "sect" or as a "catholic" body; both are necessary, and thus, Maddox highlights Methodism's embodiment of "dimensions" of this social grace: ecclesial unification of liturgical and sacramental practices, small group disciplines for mutual support and accountability, and "works of mercy" through which the Church is made present in the world.[30] Thus, Maddox shows us how Wesley offers an account of the relationship between the formation of holy affections and tempers and the practices of the Church as they mediate social grace. For Wesley, "Spirit and Discipline make a Christian."[31]

Given this background, we can turn to the shape of Wesley's warning in these two sermons concerning the relationship of Christians to the world, and we can see that Wesley understands the world to offer a sort of counter-formation to the development of holy affections and tempers.

25. Maddox, *Responsible Grace*, 69.

26. Maddox, *Responsible Grace*, 69.

27. Maddox, *Responsible Grace*, 69.

28. Maddox, "Wesley's Prescription," 18.

29. Maddox, "Social Grace," 131–60.

30. Maddox, "Social Grace," 133–35.

31. Wesley, "Causes of the Inefficacy of Christianity," §7, *Works*, 4:90.

Again, Wesley is clear that friendship with the world will not immediately cause sinful behavior among the Methodists, but this does not mean that the world is no less a dangerous influence, inasmuch as the world will "by imperceptible degrees, make you less heavenly minded."[32] But in both sermons, Wesley also uses language that leads to the conclusion that engagement with the world "directly tends to corrupt the heart," which is to say, it negatively impacts the formation of holy tempers and affections.[33] He goes on to describe the danger that friendship with the world entails:

> It tends to create in us all that pride and self-sufficiency, all that fretfulness and resentment, yea, every irregular passion and wrong disposition which are indulged . . . it gently leads . . . into habitual self-indulgence. . . . It draws [us] back into the love of the world, into foolish and hurtful desires.[34]

And this love of the world supplants holy tempers with "every other evil passion and temper of which the human soul is capable."[35] In fact, in both sermons, Wesley likens the negative influence of the world on the Methodist Christian to the transmission of disease, literally, the "distemper" that imperceptibly, yet effectively, takes root in the body and spirit.[36]

The alarm that Wesley sounds in these sermons is striking, but in the end, it does not preclude engagements between Methodists and the world that are necessary. "It would not suffice," Wesley writes, "to turn recluses, to shut ourselves up in monasteries or nunneries," because for the most practical reasons, at a minimum, "we must have some intercourse with ungodly men [sic] in order to procure the necessaries of life."[37] However, beyond this, Wesley also suggests that the engagements with the world are also motivated by what we might call evangelistic concern. Wesley suggests that "it is indeed with a good design, and from a real desire of promoting the glory of God, that many [Methodists] admit of familiar conversation with men [sic] that know not God."[38] While the term does not appear in Wesley's text, the activity he describes clearly resembles the practice of evangelism:

32. Wesley, "In What Sense," §16, *Works,* 3:149.

33. Wesley, "On Friendship," §16, *Works,* 3:134.

34. Wesley, "On Friendship," §16, *Works,* 3:134.

35. Wesley, "In What Sense," §12, *Works,* 3:147–48.

36. Wesley, "On Friendship," §17, *Works,* 3:134–35; "In What Sense," §15, *Works,* 3:149.

37. Wesley, "In What Sense," §4, *Works,* 3:145.

38. Wesley, "In What Sense," §19, *Works,* 3:151.

"You have a hope of awakening them out of sleep, and persuading them to seek the things that make for their peace."[39] Again, here we see Wesley drawing from his confidence in God's grace for all creation that works for the pardon and healing of all, including the restoration of all holy tempers. Methodists are called into the world not only because they must engage the world for the sake of business, but also for the sake of evangelistic mission.

Yet, Wesley clearly places this invitation alongside his warning that in this engagement much is at stake, "for if you do not raise their hearts up to heaven, they will draw yours down to earth."[40] Dwelling with those formed not in holy tempers and affections, Wesley warns, is a great risk, for "by this means more than any other, yea, than by all others put together, are the people called Methodists likely to lose their strength and become like other men [sic]."[41] Thus, much of the work Wesley does in these sermons is to articulate the conditions of these engagements pertaining to relationships with others in business, within families, and even in the context of marriage. While some of these admonitions would appear to be somewhat severe today, they communicate the depth of concern Wesley felt for the influence of the world on the People called Methodist. He ends the later sermon with this warning:

> Hear this, all ye that are called Methodists. However importuned or tempted thereto, have no friendship with the world. Look round and see the melancholy effects it has produced among your brethren! . . . O "come out from among them," from all unholy men [sic] . . . "and be ye separate!"[42]

In other words, while the engagement with the world is unquestionably necessary, it is an engagement that must be carefully considered and cautiously managed.

What should be clear at this point is that a Wesleyan understanding of the world must lean both ways at once. At the same time, this very stance also defines Methodist relationship to and with the world in evangelistic mission. This is to say that Wesley encouraged Methodists to acknowledge the simultaneous goodness and sinfulness that characterize the creation, and in turn, to maintain simultaneously a faithful distance from and a missional engagement with it.

39. Wesley, "In What Sense," §19, *Works*, 3:151.
40. Wesley, "In What Sense," §19, *Works*, 3:151.
41. Wesley, "In What Sense," §19, *Works*, 3:151.
42. Wesley, "On Friendship," §28, *Works*, 3:140.

This balance has proven difficult to maintain. Recalling again from the previous chapter our consideration of Outler, we can remember that he is critical of the overly developed focus within the First and Second Great Awakenings on justification without sanctification, on personal experiences of conversion from sin at the expense of any concern for the Church and its sacraments.[43] As sin remains a deeply individual concern and not a feature of social structures, evangelism pursues conversion within the supposed locus of the problem: the heart of each person. Further development of this point would lead us to consider the division of fundamentalists and modernists, and as we shall see later in this chapter, to consider the development of modernity itself that creates the conditions for a reduction of sin to the inner, spiritual life of the individual person. Suffice it to say here that one element of this failure to balance a Wesleyan perspective is the failure to see sin as a condition that describes not only individuals, but indeed, the state of the creation.

At the same time, however, we can also point to those in the Methodist tradition who have failed to lean both ways because of their movement in another direction, namely, towards emphasizing the goodness of creation at the expense of an adequate consideration of its fallen state. In fact, it is this tendency that appears with more frequency in modern Methodist theology, and that leads to an understated view of the agency of the world as problematic for a theology of mission and evangelism. For instance, we can consider some of the reading of the tradition in John Cobb's work, such as *Grace and Responsibility*, to develop a "Wesleyan theology for today."[44]

In speaking of the creation, Cobb draws from an oft-quoted section of the third sermon in Wesley's series, "Upon our Lord's Sermon on the Mount," to show Wesley's deep concern for the goodness of God's creation. Wesley writes,

> God is in all things, and . . . we are to see the Creator in the glass of every creature; . . . we should use and look upon nothing as separate from God, which indeed is a kind of practical Atheism; but with a true magnificence of thought, survey heaven and earth and all that is therein as contained by God in the hollow of His hand, who by his intimate presence holds them all in being, who

43. Outler, *Evangelism*, 64–65.
44. Cobb, *Grace and Responsibility*.

pervades and actuates the whole created frame, and is in a true
sense the Soul of the universe.[45]

While Cobb is surely right about Wesley's commitment to the goodness of the creation as the work of the Creator, this is not the only point
Cobb wants to affirm in Wesley's theological appraisal. Reading Wesley
through a Whiteheadian panentheistic lens, Cobb sees a statement of God's
immanence, extended not only to humanity, but to the whole creation. For
Cobb, "Wesley's God, the Soul of the world," is closely identified with the
creation, a God who "pervades and actuates the whole of creation, and who
enlivens, enlightens, and liberates all people, calling them to strive toward
personal and social perfection, and empowering their efforts."[46] For Cobb,
this is an affirmation in Wesley not only that "God is in all things," but even
more, that "all things are in God."[47] While he is clear that Wesley does not
unpack the significance of this theological position, Cobb gestures toward
such an account, suggesting that a commitment to God's presence in all
creation requires an ethics in kind. Acknowledging God's literal presence in
a human neighbor, or to go further, in animals, means that "what one does
to one's neighbor one does to God also," or to put it another way, "through
service of neighbor . . . one serves God."[48]

Setting aside Cobb's panentheistic identification of God within the
world, this is an important reflection on a clearly Wesleyan teaching concerning creation: God is the Creator, God loves the good creation, and this
vision of the world should affect the way Christians live, not only in relationship with each other, but in relationship to all creation. Such concerns
are not new for Cobb, who has long been a significant voice naming and
addressing the need to offer Christian theological reflection on the modern environmental crisis.[49] What I want to note is the relative absence in

---

45. Wesley, "Sermon on the Mount, III," quoted in Cobb, *Grace and Responsibility*, 50.
Interestingly, Howard Snyder, a theologian also firmly located in the Wesleyan tradition
(but not necessarily in the lines of thought associated with Cobb's work), draws the exact
same quote from Wesley's sermon to suggest the presence of God's "wisdom" in creation.
However, this leads Snyder to a Christological reading that is quite different from Cobb's
panentheistic reading. Snyder writes, "Wesley affirmed that what God had created, pre-
serves, and cares for is being redeemed through Jesus Christ who God has 'appointed
heir of all things' (Heb 1:2)" (Snyder, "World through Wesleyan Lens," 25).

46. Cobb, *Grace and Responsibility*, 51.

47. Cobb, *Grace and Responsibility*, 54.

48. Cobb, *Grace and Responsibility*, 54.

49. In truth, this has been a significant part of nearly all of Cobb's work over the

Cobb's account of the state of creation after the fall and, more particularly, the ways in which Wesley reflects concern simultaneously for the goodness and the fallenness of creation. While Cobb's connections between process and Wesleyan/Methodist theology lead to interesting and ecologically sensitive readings of the Christian tradition, they inevitably fail to truly lean both ways at once.

Cobb's tendency to read the world in such positive light is an ongoing sign of the lack of balance in a Wesleyan and Methodist theology of creation that finds its origins earlier in the nineteenth century. In an article considering the relationship between Methodism and culture, David Bebbington follows the nineteenth-century "rise of respectability" or *embourgeoisement* in English and American Methodism, connecting it to an increasing comfort with Romanticist philosophical influences in theology and an overly positive view of the world.[50] Such moves make possible the urging of Robert Newton Flew in 1918 to contemporary British Methodist preachers to see "a vision of God affirming the world as good, as delighting in the colour and gaiety and many-sidedness of human life, ceaselessly operative as in Nature so among men [*sic*] . . . and strengthening all impulses after the pure and true and beautiful."[51] In short, in Bebbington's words, "much of the denominational leadership on both sides of the Atlantic in the twentieth century possessed a world-view that was as Romantic as it was Methodist."[52] While these changes led to Methodist involvement in "remarkable cultural achievements catering for a mass market," the question here is whether such achievements came at the expense of a Methodist vision of the world, and consequently, a vision of evangelistic mission that leans both ways at once.[53]

The significance of this question should press Methodists to seek a fully balanced view of the world as both created and fallen. To bring this

---

course of his career. See Cobb, *Is It Too Late?* and *Sustainability* for just two examples.

50. Bebbington, "Methodism and Culture," 722.

51. Flew quoted by Bebbington, "Methodism and Culture," 723.

52. Focusing on the influence of this philosophical movement on the American Methodist theologian, Borden Parker Bowne, Bebbington argues that Bowne and his students (nine of whom, Bebbington notes, were serving as Bishops in the Methodist Episcopal Church [North] in the 1920s) helped to usher in an unprecedented openness to culture among Methodists. Bebbington, "Methodism and Culture," 724.

53. Bebbington cites examples of early twentieth-century Methodist writers, visual artists, architectural achievements, and the rise of gospel music. Bebbington, "Methodism and Culture," 724–25.

conversation back to the missiological concern that started it, we see what may be at risk when the world is viewed in entirely positive terms (as the good creation) or in entirely negative terms (as the sinful, fallen world). This theological imbalance affects Methodist theology and practice of mission and evangelism, leading to the problematic under- and overstatement of the Church/World difference I have tried to name as present in contemporary works. Going forward, I will argue that in order to strike this balance more effectively, a deeper study and appreciation of the world's identity and agency as both good *and* fallen will be required. Thus, in the following section, I will develop our understanding of the world, and more particularly, the activity particular to the world of principalities and powers. Reflecting Wesley's concern for the formative power of the world on the People called Methodist, this consideration of the world's agency will be crucial. In turn, this examination will allow us to consider problems in the understated and overstated accounts of the Church/World distinction in theologies of evangelism, seeking to develop a Methodist theology and practice that leans both ways at once.

The World's Identity: Principalities and Powers

Limited space precludes a lengthy description of the New Testament's understanding of the world as the realm of principalities and powers, much less an exhaustive discussion of contemporary theologians' differing interpretations of that understanding. Given the focus of this chapter, primary attention will be given to the issue of the agency attributed to the world of principalities and powers, and to their capacity to shape imagination and, in turn, perception.

There are, however, a set of commitments common to many accounts of the powers, and it is worthwhile to delineate them briefly here. In short, the biblical witness affirms that the powers are created by God and as such are given a vocation within creation that God called "good." This is to say that the powers serve a calling and are given an agency to mediate God's creative work to make and to sustain the Creation through the provision of "regularity, system, [and] order."[54] While authors may differ over how closely we can map the principalities and powers on to material forms of social life, and over the relationship of the spiritual and the material in such a map, we can simply suggest here, with Charles Campbell, that "the

54. Yoder, *Politics of Jesus*, 141.

structures and institutions of the world—political, economic, social—including the spirit or driving force that animates them, are part of God's *good* creation."[55] These powers, embodied in institutions and systems, are necessary, "they are essential to the social character of our life together, and we cannot live without them."[56] Again, from the perspective of their agency, the principalities and powers originally served a divine vocation: to echo the parental, providential care of the Father that sustained the creation.[57]

While created and while deemed good by their Creator, the powers' "echoing function" was brought to an end in the Fall.[58] New Testament discussions of the principalities and powers describe how they abandoned their vocation to "enable humanity to live a genuinely free, loving life," and instead sought to take God's place within the creation, establishing themselves as worthy of human worship and service.[59] As Yoder says, "these structures which were supposed to be our servants have become our masters and our guardians."[60] In other words, as Campbell says, "the powers have become demonic."[61]

This transformation contributes significantly to the human experience of the disorder within creation, as the powers seek their own survival and success, competing with one another for domination and, in turn, allowing the world to seem as if "all hell has broken loose."[62] As Stringfellow describes them, the principalities and powers are "legion," inasmuch as they constitute much of what humans experience as life in the world. In his prophetic, polemical style, he offers readers an extensive set of examples. The principalities and powers include

> all institutions, all ideologies, all images, all movements, all causes, all corporations, all bureaucracies, all traditions, all methods and routines, all conglomerates, all races, all nations, all idols. Thus,

55. Campbell, *Word Before the Powers*, 22.

56. Campbell, *Word Before the Powers*, 22.

57. Hendrik Berkhof makes this connection when he suggests that the powers "are the linkage between God's love and visible human experience. They are to hold life together, preserving it within God's love, serving as aids to bind men [sic] in His fellowship; intermediaries, not as barriers but as bonds between God and man" (Berkhof, *Christ and the Powers*, 29).

58. Yoder, *Politics of Jesus*, 141.

59. Yoder, *Politics of Jesus*, 143.

60. Yoder, *Politics of Jesus*, 141.

61. Campbell, *Word Before the Powers*, 25.

62. Campbell, *Word Before the Powers*, 25.

the Pentagon or the Ford Motor Company or Harvard University
... or the Diners Club or the Olympics or the Methodist Church or
the Teamsters Union are all principalities. So are capitalism, Mao-
ism, humanism, Mormonism, astrology, the Puritan work ethic,
science and scientism, white supremacy, patriotism, plus many,
many more—sports, sex, any profession or discipline, technology,
money, the family—beyond any prospect of full enumeration.[63]

However, while Stringfellow is hard-pressed to speak positively about
any of these, we cannot say that all organizations, institutions, and systems
are completely demonic. They are, however, like all principalities and powers, living between the now and the not yet, always both created and fallen,
called by God yet still sinful, and finally on the way to complete redemption. At a minimal level, God continues to rely on the powers to fulfill a
conserving function within creation, establishing a basic order necessary
for the continuation of life. At the same time, the principalities and powers, like individuals, must find themselves along the *via salutis*, repentantly
turning away from the temptation to serve gods other than God, and increasingly embodying the holiness of heart and life revealed in Jesus Christ
and empowered by the Holy Spirit.

This situation does not, however, minimize the difficulty of navigating life amid these many principalities and powers. In these circumstances
Campbell notes, "it is no wonder people feel pulled in so many directions,
almost torn apart by the powers' competing, often contradictory calls for
loyalty and service."[64] The result of this confusion is the sustained experience of "conflict and chaos" in the world.[65] But how do the powers achieve
this result? This is to ask, what agency do they possess, what work do they
do? With these authors, I argue that the fallen principalities and powers
exercise a formative agency within Creation, shaping the imagination and

63. Stringfellow, *Ethic for Christians*, 78.

64. Campbell, *Word Before the Powers*, 25–26.

65. Campbell, *Word Before the Powers*, 26. Campbell quotes Stringfellow on this issue
as well. Stringfellow writes, "[People] are veritably besieged, on all sides, at every moment simultaneously by these claims and strivings of the various powers, each seeking to
dominate, usurp, or take a person's time, attention, abilities, effort; each grasping at life
itself; each demanding idolatrous service and loyalty." Stringfellow goes on to note that
"in such a tumult it becomes very difficult for a human being even to identify the idols
which would possess him [or her]" (Campbell, *Word Before the Powers*, 13; Stringfellow,
Ethic for Christians, 90).

perception of the world in ways that drive the world to serve the selfish interests of the powers for survival.[66]

Stringfellow names several "stratagems" employed by the fallen powers for this formative purpose, and these are refined further by Campbell for an intra-ecclesial audience of preachers.[67] To shape people into servants, the disobedient powers employ negative sanctions, rewards and promises, isolation and division, demoralization and diversion, public rituals (to underwrite the division of dominant and subordinate relationships), surveillance (not only by the state but also by marketers, as described below), and secrecy. Most significant is Campbell's consideration of the sinful powers' trivialization of images and language, remaking symbols and "inverting" language in order to obscure truth. "In the place of truthful speech," Campbell argues, "we encounter the propaganda of the state, the exaggerations of Madison Avenue, the doublespeak of politicians and advertisers, the false claims of expertise by bureaucrats, the code language of racism, and the diversions of the entertainment industry."[68]

The use of language and image in these ways has a formative effect, Campbell argues, shaping human imagination in a particular way, which in turn affects our actions, because "how we see the world shapes how we live in it."[69] More directly stated, this formation consists of an attempt to keep human imagination and perception functioning in an unconscious fashion, anesthetizing our ability to realize that things are not as they should be. Stringfellow articulates this "goal" most effectively when he suggests that the powers seek the "immobilization or surrender or destruction of the mind" and the "neutralization or abandonment or demoralization of the conscience," all of which result in the death of any rational perception or moral action. Through the various means they employ, the powers function to shape the ways in which we both see and describe the world.

66. A fuller account would have to complicate the portrayal here to name and exemplify powers and principalities in the world that serve their divine vocation faithfully, or more explicitly, who struggle more with the calling to turn from serving death to serving the God of life. In other words, some powers and principalities, some organizations and institutions, are holier than others. That this is the case allows, for example, Karl Barth's location of instructive examples of faithfulness outside of the Church in the world, in the secular parables. See Barth, *CD* 4/3.1:114–24.

67. Stringfellow, *Ethic for Christians*, chapter 4; Campbell, *Word Before the Powers*, 33–43.

68. Campbell, *Word Before the Powers*, 40. Of course, Campbell could also point to the ways the Church itself as a fallen power is also sometimes guilty of such stratagems.

69. Campbell, *Word Before the Powers*, 42.

The World's Agency: Principalities, Powers, and Formation

Wesley's concern for Methodists was that the engagement with the world would lead to "distemper," or a malformed set of affections and tempers that would undermine the integrity of a holy life. If we are called to the holiness of heart and life that reflects the proper formation of affections and tempers, and if we can agree with Stringfellow (as we saw in the previous section) that the principalities and powers of the world function with an agency that resists Christian identity and action and that truly serves not God but rather death, then we must seek a deeper understanding of the ways in which this agency exercises formative power. In short, in the effort to construct a Methodist theology of evangelism, we must articulate the counter-formation to holiness, the agency of the world's principalities and powers that would invite Methodists to serve an evangelistic mission other than the one shaped inside the *missio Dei*.

In addressing this issue, I will turn in this section to two contemporary authors who can thicken our understanding of the times in which we live, and of the formative agency of the world, the principalities and powers, at work among us. In an article written at the end of the twentieth century, "Messiah's People: The Culture of the Church in the Midst of the Nations,"[70] David Yeago reflects on the state of the Church in relationship to the world as revealed during the development of modernity and offers us a lens through which we are able to see the imagination-shaping work of the powers. More specifically, Yeago draws our attention to the shaping power of the late-capitalist market in North American cultures—a power that Vincent Miller will later examine in his own work, *Consuming Religion: Christian Faith and Practice in a Consumer Culture*.[71] Indeed, Miller's analysis further clarifies the formative influence of the powers and principalities located in the contemporary market and in the consumer culture that serves it. Together, the two authors show us in greater detail the "imaginary" that the market in a fallen world creates and that pervasively and even unconsciously operates to distort human perception and action, exercising within the Church the constant temptation to serve the market through a focus on the individual shaped by late-modern consumer culture. Indeed, what I hope we shall see through the contributions of Yeago and Miller is the deep, almost imperceptible pull toward a tendency to limit

---

70. Yeago, "Messiah's People," 146–71.

71. Miller, *Consuming Religion*.

our theological-practical imagination, leading to the development of a theology of evangelism dominated by concern for relevance, legitimacy, and success, instead of by a concern for faithfulness in witness.

The Powers of Modernity and Market

In his article, Yeago begins with a historical account, noting that the eventual fusion of the divided Church(es) with various nation-states in the post-Reformation period created the environment that led to the European wars of religion. In turn, these years of "misery" fueled the development of the Enlightenment and the creation of a rationality, which became known as "secular," distinct from that which was offered by the "sacred" traditions. Religious descriptions were supplanted by the supposed discovery of what Yeago calls a "more basic 'secular' account which was always there underneath."[72] Further, these descriptions were not considered to be equal, yet differing accounts of reality, or simply rival traditions offering different perspectives on the same phenomena; rather, Yeago argues, the sacred was the "varnish" on reality that could be "scraped off" to discover the more fundamental, secular, or natural truth. So described, this more basic account of truth as natural represented an "understanding of reality we all have in common, transcending all our divisive particularities, including religious ones."[73]

With this development, the stage was set for further distinguishing the sacred and the secular within this emerging modernity as their split was mapped onto the corresponding differentiation between the "public" and the "private." In this "modern settlement," the secular is rendered as outward public reality, while the sacred traditions are relegated to the interior world of the private individual or sect. Thus banished from an existence that could be considered "outside of" or "different from" that larger public, secular reality, the Church was consequently reduced to being a "private 'voluntary association' of like-minded individuals *within* a public order governed by secular rationality."[74] As such, the Church is then set in a per-

72. Yeago, "Messiah's People," 147.

73. Yeago, "Messiah's People," 148.

74. Yeago argues that in the modern settlement, the Church is not "allowed" to be what he calls "a distinctive public community in its own right, the present civic assembly of the eschatological city, constituting a new public order which occupies its own public space in the midst of the nations" (Yeago, "Messiah's People," 148).

petual struggle to discover its purpose, its "reason for being," within the boundaries of that secular space, and thus, is also subject to defining those aims in light of the "projects and aspirations of that larger order."[75] This perpetual struggle for purpose has been described by Reinhard Hütter as the Church's "ceaseless crisis of legitimation."[76]

So, in other words, with the acceptance of the relationship of "public" and "secular" in modernity, the Church was allowed to occupy the space that was left over: the private sector, where the Church can be a voluntary association of individuals involved in religion, much as the Rotary Club is a voluntary association of individuals involved in business. However, Yeago goes further, arguing that in this modern settlement, the Church as a voluntary association of individuals involved in religion had to define the shape of that involvement in ways that could remain intelligible within that larger secular order. To put it another way, the Church will make sense in modernity only if and just to the extent that it has a function that somehow serves the secular order. "Thus," Yeago writes,

> the problem of the Church's mission is defined as the problem of the *relevance* of the ideas and values, the message, or the religious experience which the Church conveys to the particular larger culture of which the Church is a part. What role could these ideas, this message, this experience play within this culture? How could they be "meaningful" in this cultural setting? What legitimate place could they find there? What function could they fulfill in the life of the surrounding culture?[77]

Usually, Yeago argues, this means that the Church "figures only as the vehicle for something essentially disembodied and non-public: a set of beliefs and values, an abstract 'message,' an inward religious experience"[78] and not a public, visible community that constitutes a different way of living in the world, but not being "of the world."

Thus, in that search to be "relevant," the modern Church then most often turns to one of the two forms of recognized "public life" in liberal societies—the state or the market. If they turn to the state, the Churches tend to take on relevance in relationship to the social and political projects also being pursued in the context of the state. "That is, the Church can seek

75. Yeago, "Messiah's People," 149.
76. Yeago, "Messiah's People," 149.
77. Yeago, "Messiah's People," 149.
78. Yeago, "Messiah's People," 148.

a reason for being by associating itself with one or another of the parties and movements which seek to influence the state and get its monopoly of coercive power behind their own agendas."[79] In other words, "the Church legitimates itself by taking on the socially recognized role of a motivational support-system for socio-political struggle."[80]

However, in turning to the market, the Church accepts the role of becoming another "provider of goods and services to consumers" without realizing that the market is "governed by the principle of subjective value: goods and services have whatever value consumers choose, for whatever reason, to place upon them. This means that legitimacy in the culture of the market is identical with market share."[81] Under these conditions, Yeago argues, the Church cannot but determine its legitimacy based on the measure of "consumer response," and more specifically on the percentage of the total "religion-market" that it can attract and serve.[82]

I would argue that it is this latter formation within the dominant market that has most influenced contemporary theology and practice of evangelism, and that it is most evident among those who I suggest tend to understate the importance of the Church/World relationship. Yet, we can say more here, to be more explicit about the relationship between the identity and agency of the powers in the contemporary market and the ways in which this relationship influences the identity and the agency of the Church, and more specifically, the theology and practice of evangelism in the Church. To expand that description and to make those connections more explicitly, I turn now to Vincent Miller's *Consuming Religion: Christian Faith and Practice in a Consumer Culture*.[83] Miller's analysis further clarifies the formative influence of the powers and principalities located in the contemporary market and the consumer culture that serves it.

In his book, Miller offers us an account of the rise of capitalism and the transformation in life it brought to the US in the nineteenth and twentieth centuries. With the advent of the "Fordist" Era, social reality began to change concomitantly with the shift from production to consumption in the national economy. In this economic reality, the decline of the self-sustaining household made room for the development of the single-family

79. Yeago, "Messiah's People," 165.
80. Yeago, "Messiah's People," 166.
81. Yeago, "Messiah's People," 166.
82. Yeago, "Messiah's People," 167.
83. Miller, *Consuming Religion*.

home, which, Miller argues, represented "a milestone in the shunting of the need for social standing into consumption in a way that ensures the endless perpetuation of consumer desire."[84] The emergence of the single-family home allowed society to reduce its commitment to the multi-generational family in lieu of a narrow focus upon the maintenance of the nuclear family. This family sought an autonomous lifestyle, increasingly insulated from extended family and other social connections, and was sustained by the security of wages (rather than the support of the extended family and community) and by new technologies that sustained a household for the smaller family unit. Miller points out that this shift to an increasingly isolated existence fueled by consumption represented one of the thickest roots beneath what would sprout as the modern woes of advanced capitalism and consumer culture: individualism, materialism, and the decreasing capacity to care well for one another.[85] Part of this care, of course, includes the formative role elder generations offer to younger generations, which is mitigated as generations in the extended family are separated from one another by the move to the nuclear family. As Miller puts it, this shift created a norm wherein "each generation is freer to make its own choices regarding cultural and religious practices from the options they encounter. These choices of culture are increasingly drawn from commercial offerings as consumption becomes a means of establishing and expressing identity."[86]

This effect intensifies over the course of the twentieth century, as the alienation of the single-family home was exacerbated in the Post-Fordist Era, beginning in the 1970s. In this period of economic instability, facing diminishing returns from mass-market production, advanced capitalism shifted into new strategies to sustain the cycle of production and consumption vital to the ongoing functionality of the economic system. While some of these strategies involved changes to the systems of labor and production, my interest is in the developments made to increase consumption. The primary strategy serving this end was the development of the niche market.

---

84. Miller, *Consuming Religion*, 50.

85. Miller writes, "The individualism and materialism rightly condemned by papal encyclicals, ethicists, and cultural critics have their foundation in the very material social structure of the single-family home." And thus, being isolated from the neighborhood, the community, and even the welfare of others in the world, the "geography of the single family home makes it very likely that we will care more about the feeding of our pets than about the millions of children who go to bed hungry around us" (Miller, *Consuming Religion*, 51).

86. Miller, *Consuming Religion*, 53.

Flexibility in production methods allowed the development of specialized products for particular groups of people, identified by the growing capacity of information technology to make finer distinctions of desires within varying demographics.[87] This specialization had an even more fragmentary effect upon society. While the move to the single-family home created the socially isolated nuclear family, the development of targeted niche marketing carried that disintegration even further, considering each member of the nuclear family a viable consumer to whom marketing could be directed. Further individualized, each member of the nuclear family was empowered to make consumer choices as an individual, for him/herself. These choices were made apart from consideration of the needs of others, separated not just from those in the extended family or in the wider community (local and global), but even from those "others" who lived under the same roof.[88]

While this narrative explains the rise of a nation of consumers, Miller also displays how such a consumer culture affects the appropriation and practice of religious traditions. The market excels at developing different products, commodities especially shaped for each niche in order to maximize the potential for sales and profits. In that environment, the market will take anything and everything that it can in order to package it and offer it as a "new" product to the public so that almost no line is drawn around that which cannot be subjected to commodification and consumption—including of course, all forms of culture, religious and otherwise. In fact, "the most profound challenge of consumerism," as Miller puts it "[is] the commodification of culture—the reduction of religious beliefs, symbols, and values to objects of consumption."[89] Such beliefs, symbols, values, and practices, Miller explains,

> are abstracted from their conditions of production, presented as objects valuable in themselves, shorn of their interrelations with

---

87. As an example of this development, Miller offers the story of the H. J. Heinz Company that in the Fordist era built its reputation in the mustard market with its signature square-faceted jar and familiar label and logo: it sold its singular product on the basis of its reputation. In the Post-Fordist era, however, Heinz began to develop new kinds of mustard, most notably Grey Poupon, which fed a market of young professionals (Yuppies) seeking a more gourmet experience not offered by the plain yellow mustard they ate while growing up. Miller quotes a subject from another study on post-Fordist capitalism: "All I want is a place where I can buy twelve kinds of mustard" (Miller, *Consuming Religion*, 67–68).

88. Miller, *Consuming Religion*, 70.

89. Miller, *Consuming Religion*, 19.

the other symbols, beliefs, and practices that determine their meaning, and function in their traditional contexts. Unmoored from these contexts, their "semantic mass" is greatly reduced. Cultural commodities become more susceptible to manipulation and misappropriation, free-floating signifiers that can be put to uses unrelated, indeed contradictory, to the meanings they bear.[90]

Thus, individuals inside and outside of the Christian tradition are able to purchase a crucifix, either because it is an item of devotion and prayer, or because they agree with the popular musical artist Madonna and her claim that "Crucifixes are sexy."[91] The point here is to note how even these religious symbols, beliefs, and practices are subject to the very commodification that allows for their purchase by individuals in the consumer culture. Being so formed by the powers, these individuals become the focus for the deliberation of congregations that seek the legitimacy found in consumer popularity, which is, as Yeago reminds us, the highest measure of contemporary cultural relevance.

Because this is the story within which we find ourselves, Miller suggests that theology and theological reflection on ecclesial practices must take these realities into account. As he puts it, "theology must consider the systems that present elements of tradition in a commodified fashion and the formation of believers' interpretive habits that incline them to engage tradition as a commodity."[92] Indeed, Miller suggests that, for these very reasons, even interaction within our religious traditions is a dangerous task. This is so because, due to the pervasive nature of the market's formation of consumer culture, we, too, will be subject to the same tendency to commodify aspects of our own tradition. It will even be a temptation for us to take such traditional symbols, beliefs, and practices and to abstract them, to reify them, and to place them in service to a goal that seems worthy to us and good for the numerical growth of the Church. Yet, all of this may be perpetuating the problem to which Yeago points, namely, the continuing eclipse of the Church in the acceptance of the modern settlement, the Church serving the market by seeking relevance that is actually catering to the individual shopper.

The developments described by Yeago and Miller give more texture to the situation in which we find ourselves as Christians. Through their

90. Miller, *Consuming Religion,* 66.

91. Miller, *Consuming Religion,* 79.

92. Miller, *Consuming Religion,* 66.

work, we come to see in greater detail the imaginary that pervasively and even unconsciously operates in ways that distort our perception and our actions, exercising within the Church the constant temptation to serve the market through a focus on the individual shaped by late-modern consumer culture. Indeed, what I hope we see through the contributions of Yeago and Miller is the deep, almost imperceptible pull of a market-based concern for relevance, legitimacy, and success that limits both our theological-practical imagination and theology of evangelism and diverts our attention away from a concern for faithfulness.

The World's Influence in Evangelism

Yeago and Miller have clarified the formative agency of the principalities and powers by focusing upon the particular context of the late-modern, North American/North Atlantic market. Now we turn more explicitly to see how these moves affect the account developing here. In this section, I will recall the argument from chapter 1 that some theologies of evangelism tend to understatement of the theological differentiation of Church and world. However, given our engagement with the Methodist tradition, the lack of a balanced theology of creation that takes into account both the goodness and the fallenness of the world, and our further investigation into the agency of the world in that fallenness, embodied in the principalities and the powers and more specifically in the contemporary market, we are situated to say more explicitly what is problematic about the understatement present in contemporary theology of evangelism. Simply put, without a robust account of the agency of the world within the Church/World distinction, theologies of evangelism will fail to keep a balance that leans both ways at once.

Those who understate the Church/World difference often neglect the formative impact of the world inside the Church (reflecting Wesley's concern for the formation of a sanctified People called Methodist), and in that neglect, fail to offer an account of ecclesial formation as crucial to the evangelistic engagement with that fallen-yet-redeemed world. A lack of concern for the agency of the principalities and powers undermines the possibility of a theology of evangelism that can faithfully navigate the Church/World relationship.

This insight should clarify my engagement in chapter 1 with Hunter's work, which I judged exemplary of the understatement of Church/World.

For example, I believe that the analyses offered here point to the ways in which the world may influence the development of evangelistic mission. In particular, in Hunter's positing of "tradition" versus "mission," and in the recommendation of the "SLAM" method for the contextualization or inculturation of the Church's practices, there is little, if any, consideration of the ways in which adapting to "the style, the language, the aesthetics, and the music of the target population" may or may not be capitulations to the powers and principalities active in the shaping of each.[93]

While Hunter does suggest that "at a deeper level," the Church's seeking of an effective evangelistic outreach will have to engage the "core attitudes, beliefs, and values that provide the . . . 'worldview' through which the society views the world," there is no sign that what disciplines Hunter's concern is a view of that world in biblical terms, as the fallen, yet redeemed creation of powers and principalities.[94] On the contrary, Hunter places the focus on the world as it is known and experienced by those outside the Church as the primary model for the adaptation of ecclesial practice. In this light, the world for Hunter functions as a neutral context, the field within which evangelism takes place, without concern for the agency at work therein.

Yet, given what we have learned from Stringfellow, Yeago, and Miller, we are led to ask, how will the Church know whether the view of the "world" imported into the Church and used to shape the practices of evangelism, formation, and worship conforms to the way of Jesus or the disobedient principalities of the world? In other words, under these terms, how can the Church know which Lord it serves—the Lord Jesus or the lords of this world?

At this point, it should be said that it is important to acknowledge that the Church and its practices are always embodied in a local context, and thus, are subject to the necessary practices of contextualization and enculturation. While the tendency to understate the differentiation of Church

---

93. As a reminder, Hunter writes, "At the surface level, an indigenous ministry strategy involves adapting to the style, the language, the aesthetics, and the music of the target population. (SLAM serves as a convenient acronym.) At a deeper level, indigenous ministry involves engaging the attitudes, beliefs, and values characteristic of the society, especially the core attitudes, beliefs, and values that provide the lens, or the 'worldview' through which the society views the world" (Hunter, *Radical Outreach*, 33). Yet, when Hunter speaks of "the world," his concern is not the identity and agency of the world in biblical terms, as expressed in the work of Berkhof, Yoder, and Stringfellow.

94. Hunter, *Radical Outreach*, 33.

and world in a theology of evangelism can lead to the unquestioned importation of the practices of a given context into the Church, it is not a question whether this engagement will have to take place; the Church is always located in a place, and whether for the sake of evangelism or formation or worship, will have to address the question of intelligibility in that place. Just to this extent, Hunter's suggestions are well taken, if not for their substance, then for their challenge: the Church is always embodied in a context.

Even so, the issue being raised here is the need to attend to the terms of the Church's engagement with the world. While the recommendation is for a missional ecclesiology that posits the Church as always leaning into its tradition and practices as well as into the world in reconciling mission, this ecclesiology can only be established through a robust consideration of the differing agencies of both Church and world. In these terms, the need to ask these questions concerning relevance and Hunter's recommendations for adaptation within context are understandable, but do not go deep enough or far enough to offer a theology of evangelism that maintains counterbalance. Unfortunately, without adequate consideration of the agency of the world, Hunter offers a theology and practice of evangelism that leans just one way—into the world, without enough concern for the possibility that in that leaning, the Church can lose itself in the process.

Conclusion

William Stringfellow argued that without consideration of the identity and the agency of the principalities and powers, "there can be no serious, realistic, or biblical comprehension of the witness of the Church in the world."[95] We have taken up the implicit challenge posed here through the consideration of the identity and agency associated with the powers and their formative capacity to disrupt Wesleyan holiness and evangelism. I have argued that a properly Methodist theology of evangelism will seek a balanced vision of the world that understands the necessity and the danger of evangelistic mission within a creation that is simultaneously fallen, disobedient, and yet, created as good and yearning for redemptive fulfillment. But with this account in place, understanding more clearly the challenge posed by the world, we turn next to consider the Church along the way toward an account of evangelistic witness that leans both ways at once. To be the Church and, at the same time, to be fully located in and engaged with

95. Stringfellow, *Free in Obedience*, 51–52.

the world will require consideration of the Church's identity and agency. We begin that work in the next chapter.

3

The Church

Christian evangelism requires as a condition of its very possibility the presence in the world, though distinct from the world, of a visible people, a new society, into which persons may be invited and formed . . . [the] neglect of Peoplehood may well be the central challenge facing Christian evangelism.[1]

Introduction

TURNING FROM CONSIDERATION OF the identity and the agency of the world, in the final two chapters, I will ask: what is the shape of Methodist ecclesiology and evangelism that is "in but not of" this world? If the theological differentiation of Church and world is crucial for a theology of evangelism, we are left with the need to say more about the identity of such a Church in the world. Taking that up in this chapter, I argue that developing an account of the Church begins with the assertion of the Church's identity defined as a particular "People" called "Methodist."

In the development and provision of the *General Rules of the United Societies* in 1743, Wesley envisioned, formed, and sustained the formation of a particular People in the Methodist movement.[2] I believe this sense of "Peoplehood" is crucial to Methodist ecclesiological identity, and it is from *within* this understanding of Methodism as a People that we should view

1. Stone, *Evangelism after Christendom*, 194–95.
2. Wesley, "General Rules," *Works*, 9:69–75.

a Methodist expression of evangelistic mission, shaping a movement for individual and social reform that requires location in a visible, practicing, and witnessing community of discipleship. Such Peoplehood constitutes the basis for a missional ecclesiology that embodies a set of evangelistic practices and structures aimed at shaping transformed lives and a transformed world, leaning into the traditions and practices of the Christian tradition as well as into the needs of the world, both ways at once.

Considering Wesleyan Ecclesiology

Consideration of the Church's identity inside the Wesleyan and Methodist tradition begins with John Wesley. Wesley drew together disparate streams within Christian tradition in order to develop an ecclesiology described as a "creative synthesis."[3] Of course, his location and training make clear the influence of the Anglican tradition, and particularly the Anglican *via media* that mediates the tensions between the Catholic tradition and Reform Protestant influences.[4] This stream was joined, however, by a second, broadly sourced, but essentially acknowledged as the influence of Continental Pietism, particularly in the Moravian tradition.[5]

While Wesley learned the essentials of Church order and practice from his own upbringing and training in the English Church (consequently believing that it was in the forms of the English Church that one came the closest to the faithful incarnation of the practices of the early Church), it was from the Pietists that Wesley came to see the power of *ecclesiolae in ecclesia*, the movement of intentional communities of Christians within the larger, established Church seeking reformation, restoration, and renewal.[6] In this tradition, renewal was nurtured in the formation of small groupings, the *ecclesiolae* which Howard Snyder describes as "voluntary sub communit[ies] providing the option of a more deeply earnest experience of

---

3. Maddox, *Responsible Grace*, 241. Albert Outler wrote, "John Wesley's own doctrine of the Church, like the rest of his theology, was an interesting amalgam." See Outler, "Do Methodists Have a Doctrine of the Church?," 14.

4. Maddox, *Responsible Grace*, 241.

5. Kenneth Collins has argued that "Wesley's ecclesiology is unintelligible apart from [Pietist and Moravian] contributions" (Collins, *Theology of John* Wesley, 247). See Maddox, *Responsible Grace*, 241. For an in-depth study of these relationships, see also Snyder, *Pietism, Moravianism, and Methodism*.

6. Collins, *Theology of John Wesley*, 247–8.

the Christian faith for those believers who sense such a need."[7] The power of small groupings of Christians for the purpose of mutual support, shared discipline, and community accountability provided a vision of authentic Christian life. But the renewal movement retained its location inside the body of the Church, expressions of the Church (*ecclesia*) in smaller, focused gatherings for practice and renewal (*ecclesiolae*). Such an arrangement has informed some definitions of Methodist ecclesial identity. For example, as Albert Outler put it in his essay from the 1962 Oxford Institute, "Do Methodists Have a Doctrine of the Church?," Methodism functioned as an "evangelical order" within the Church catholic, a movement focused on the formation of holiness of heart and life.[8]

Focus on the formation of holiness as a central concern determining Methodist ecclesial identity seems consistent with Wesley's own reflections on the relationship of mission and structure in the Methodist movement. Wesley believed that God raised the people called Methodist for the purpose of "reform[ing] the nation, particularly the Church, and . . . spread[ing] scriptural holiness over the land."[9] Wesley connects this missional clarity to answer questions related to the shape of the Church when he asks, "What is the end of all ecclesiastical order? Is it not to bring souls from the power of Satan to God; and to build them up in his fear and love?"[10] And in answer to his own question, he says, "Order, then, is so far valuable, as it answers these ends; and if it answers them not, it is nothing worth."[11]

Such a comment reflects what one scholar has called an "insoluble tension" in Wesley's ecclesiology between the pragmatic development of the Methodist movement as an organization focused on the purpose of Christian formation and spiritual renewal on the one hand, and a "lasting high-Church sacramentalism" that keeps Wesley tethered to the Church of England, on the other.[12] Even so, while this explains the formation of the organizational structures and practices that characterized early Methodism, this same dynamic drove Wesley to an even greater ecclesial adaptation later in his life, namely when he makes the extraordinary decision to ordain new leaders for North American Methodist ministry. Such a clear

7. Snyder, *Pietism, Moravianism, and Methodism,* 15.

8. Outler, "Do Methodists Have a Doctrine of the Church?," 13.

9. Wesley, "Large Minutes," 299.

10. Wesley, "Letter to 'John Smith,'" *Works,* 26:206.

11. Wesley, "Letter to 'John Smith,'" *Works,* 26:206.

12. Oh, *John Wesley's Ecclesiology,* 3.

departure from established Church order displays "the logical and inevitable outcome of Wesley's decision to place soteriological concerns above those of institutional commitments."[13] The ranked ordering of soteriological mission to institutional stability "permitted [Wesley] to accommodate the structures of worship and administration to the spiritual needs of the people he sought to serve."[14] Given Wesley's eventual embrace of ecclesial irregularities such as field preaching, transgression of parish boundaries, and—eventually—extra-ecclesial ordination, it seems an evident conclusion that Wesley embraced ecclesial adaptation, but just to the extent that it served the extension of Methodist mission, understood as reform and renewal for the sake of shaping holiness.

Wesley's willingness to adapt ecclesial structure and practice for the sake of extending soteriological mission continues to inform contemporary Methodist ecclesiology and missiology. George Hunter, for example, suggests that Wesley was "an unapologetic pragmatist" when it came to questions of ecclesial organization for the sake of evangelistic mission, emphasizing that the "the supreme standard for evaluating any evangelism approach was its outcomes."[15] Put simply, when it comes to the relationship between soteriological mission and ecclesial structure, a Wesleyan approach might support the conclusion that the former dictates the shape of the latter.

But now we must ask whether such a relationship should continue to inform the shape of contemporary Wesleyan or Methodist ecclesiology. While Wesley's pragmatic concerns for the formation of holiness clearly shaped Methodist organization and ecclesial adaptation, does this describe the identity of the Church for Wesley, or for those who followed him in the Methodist movements and Churches? Is the identity of the Church in the Methodist tradition best understood as a "means" in service to the telos of salvation?

I believe an overly pragmatic or instrumental understanding of the relationship of soteriology and ecclesiology leads to an understated account of the Church's identity and, in turn, the Church's agency. Put differently, the Church's identity is more than the geographic location of salvation, and the Church's agency is greater than the work of carrying the means of grace for the formation of holiness. A first step in seeking a thicker account of

13. Bence, "Salvation and the Church," 310.
14. Bence, "Salvation and the Church," 311.
15. Hunter, *To Spread the Power*, 43.

Methodist ecclesiology along these lines presses us to remember the proper relationship between Methodism and the Church.

Richard Heitzenrater considers the shape of a Wesleyan ecclesiology and seems to continue an account of practical goals driving ecclesial order when he suggests that Methodism is best understood as a "means of grace."[16] "Methodism, he writes, "is designed by Wesley to help people experience the presence of God in their lives in many different ways. Both the organization and the program of their mission are designed with this purpose in mind."[17] But Heitzenrater clearly maintains a distinction in his analysis between Methodism and the Church, consistent with the historical context within which Methodism is formed. Here, he argues,

> Wesley's view of holiness, love of God and love of neighbor, works of piety and works of mercy, using the means of grace, becomes embodied in Methodism, which he views as the place where the Church can experience the grace, presence, power of God in ways that represent genuine Christianity in its organized form—the Church.[18]

Methodism continues to be a "religious community" where "people could experience the power and presence of God's love." But he is careful to say that Methodism does not replace the Church, but instead, is a means of grace to the Church, just to the extent that it is that "part of the Church that was experiencing what the Church was intended to be."[19]

Heitzenrater's conclusion echoes Outler's own, mentioned above, framing Methodism as an "evangelical order" within the Church catholic.[20] Outler also identifies the crucial role soteriological mission plays in the formation of Methodist organization and practice, suggesting that the Methodist movement was best understood as "act" and as "mission," providing the context for the maturing of souls along the way of the *via salutis* and representing that which the Church was called to be at its best, a renewal of real Christianity embodied in the People called Methodist.[21] But he is also clear that such a rendering of Methodist ecclesial identity has to be placed within the distinction of *ecclesia* and *ecclesiola*, where Methodism is

16. Heitzenrater, "Wesleyan Ecclesiology," 119–28.

17. Heitzenrater, "Wesleyan Ecclesiology," 126.

18. Heitzenrater, "Wesleyan Ecclesiology," 126.

19. Heitzenrater, "Wesleyan Ecclesiology," 126.

20. Outler, "Do Methodists Have a Doctrine of the Church?," 13.

21. Outler, "Do Methodists Have a Doctrine of the Church?," 19.

a movement clearly focused on the formation of holiness of heart and life, but also clearly located inside the *ecclesia*.[22]

Outler and Heitzenrater rightly remind us of Wesley's and Methodism's location within the structure of the established Church. While the *ecclesiola* can improvise (to some extent) with form and content in the search for the renewal and embodiment of Christian discipline, it only remains intelligible as part of its larger body given its primary location inside the *ecclesia*. Latter-day Methodism cannot make such a claim, particularly in its North American forms. To these bodies Outler pointed his remarks in 1962, reminding them that despite Methodism's original identity as a renewal movement, the current calling of the Methodist movement in this "ad interim" period previous to renewed Christian unity is to be a Church, responsible in creed, catechism, and sacramental life to the traditions of the Church catholic.[23]

What is at stake in the question over the relationship of ecclesial order and soteriological mission is no less than the potential evacuation of Methodism's contemporary responsibility to embody its identity as a Church and the potential loss of the gift and witness that Methodism offers as part of the ecumenical whole. In other words, to favor efficacious soteriological mission in determining ecclesial order places the apostolicity and catholicity of the Church at risk.

It is tempting to emphasize Wesley's experience at Aldersgate as the primary catalyst for Methodist evangelistic mission, where the "middle Wesley" and his focus on the centrality of justification and the onset of field preaching become paradigmatic forms of a pragmatically defined Methodist ecclesiology and evangelism. Yet, we do so at the cost of learning from the "whole Wesley." This recognition is the fruit of Randy Maddox's work in his essay, "Social Grace," where he argues that the generally accepted ecclesial synthesis in Wesley was more than a practical combination of differing streams of tradition, but was, rather, a synthesis deeply based in Wesley's own theological commitments in theological anthropology, sin, and soteriology. In other words, a broader consideration of Wesley's theology leads us to a richer understanding of Wesley's understanding of the Church's identity.

We remember from the previous chapter that, for Wesley, salvation amounted to the "restoration of the soul" or "renewal" of the image of

22. Outler, "Do Methodists Have a Doctrine of the Church?," 13.
23. Outler, "Do Methodists Have a Doctrine of the Church?," 26–28.

God in holiness, a claim understandable given the background of Wesley's "moral psychology" considering the role of the "affections" and "tempers" to inform an account of human moral action.[24] Because of the corrupting effects of sin on the tempers and affections, salvation addresses the need for renewal through justification and sanctification available in the means of grace through which believers can be nurtured in the way that leads to having "the mind of Christ." This thicker sense of salvation and its relationship to the formation of holy tempers also leads us now to thicken the relationship of soteriology to ecclesiology.

In Maddox's terms, "the Church is a means of social grace for the nurturing of affections."[25] This "social grace" assumes the practices of the Church as both a sect and as a catholic body; both the *ecclesiolae* and the *ecclesia* are necessary.[26] Thus, Wesley's ecclesiological synthesis was motivated by his theological and specifically soteriological concerns for connecting believers to the means by which the healing and reshaping of the tempers and affections can take place. In short, for Wesley, "Spirit and Discipline make a Christian."[27]

This means that Methodism cannot accept a simple pragmatic relationship between ecclesial adaptation in pursuit of its soteriological mission, inasmuch as part of fulfilling this mission is the Church's sustained engagement in the traditioned practices of the Church catholic, particularly the sacraments, as instituted means of grace that are vital to the formation of holiness along the way of salvation. The necessity of ongoing formation in Wesleyan soteriology requires the sustenance of such traditioned practices.

In addition, because these practices are also irreducibly "social" or communal, any adaptation of the Church's order must be held in that light; in other words, because the salvation of Christians is a social event, mediated through the "social grace" in the Church, the Church cannot simply adapt its views on salvation or the practices of evangelistic mission in order to export saving grace separable from participation in the community of the Church itself. In this light, questions considering the adaptation of ecclesial order and practice are always questions for the whole community of the Church. The Church adapts as a community for the sake of extending community. Thus any "necessity" for changing ecclesial order for the sake

24. Maddox, "Wesley's Prescription," 18.

25. Maddox, "Social Grace," 133.

26. Maddox, "Social Grace," 133.

27. Wesley, "Causes of the Inefficacy of Christianity," §7, *Works*, 4:90.

of evangelistic mission assumes the discerning judgment and consensus of the community along the *via salutis*, as well as the conviction that such adaptation is engaged to extend the Church's reach as a communal "means of social grace for the nurturing of affections."[28] Here we see the beginnings of a thicker account of the Church's identity.

Ecclesial Identity: A People Called Methodist

Against any tendency to read the Church as the environment or context within which individuals seek salvation along the *via salutis*, salvation rightly understood is both mediated through the Church (as a means of grace) and accounts for the Church as a visible, practicing, witnessing People called Methodist. In other words, the telos of salvation is not a collection of "people called Methodists," but rather, the formation of a new community, a "People called Methodist."

What this understanding requires is resistance to the desire to posit formation prior to evangelistic mission, so that the salvation of individuals somehow results in the appearance of the Church. While an account of the Church's practices of formation is crucial to an account of ecclesial agency and to an account of evangelistic mission, the question is one of sequence. For Wesleyans, salvation simultaneously requires community and extends community, as this holy People called Methodist engage the world in evangelistic mission. While the first claim (salvation requires community) is accepted among interpreters of the tradition, it is our task to show the truth of the latter claim, namely, that in their life together, the community of the *via salutis*, the People called Methodist, embody, proclaim, witness to, and extend the salvation of Christ in evangelistic mission.

In what follows, I will suggest that we can reclaim a holistic understanding of evangelistic mission when we consider its location not as a program but as the natural display of the life of a particular "People" in the world. This sense of Peoplehood is crucial to Methodist ecclesiological identity and evangelistic mission, seeking transformed lives and a transformed world, leaning into the identity and practices of the Christian tradition as well as into the needs and concerns of the world, both ways at once.

---

28. Maddox, "Social Grace," 133.

Typologies of Ecclesial Renewal

Can we regard the Methodists as a "People"? For many, such an ecclesio-logical identification may seem an odd fit, if not a mistake. In his essay, "A People in the World," John Howard Yoder considers post-Reformation Church renewal movements in order to identify a broad ecclesiological ty-pology that he suggests repeats itself in critical periods of renewal. Accord-ing to Yoder, there are three types: the theocratic, the spiritualist, and the believers' Church, the differences between them being most significantly their differing placement of the "locus of historical meaning" and, conse-quently, the proper form of ecclesial gathering.[29]

Yoder associates the theocratic type with any effort to connect renewal of the Church to the larger renewal of society in general. The "locus of his-torical meaning" for the theocrat is "the movement of the whole society."[30] The Church seeks a role of influence either through accepting its fusion with the state itself or, in disestablished contexts, through supporting its members as they wield power in secular vocations, inviting them to do so specifically as Christians. In either case, the telos is the same: the Church sees renewal in the totalizing vision of society where all are Christians and what counts as meaningful renewal is tied intimately to the transformation of the socio-politico-economic sphere.

Yoder's second type is a reactive development to the first. The spiri-tualist type relocates the center of historical meaning from the theocratic focus on renewal in the whole society to the inner realm of the individual's spiritual life. Thus, renewal in the Church tends toward eschewing the per-ceived "cold" formal practices of the established Church and toward creat-ing para-Church forms that encourage and support the inward experience of vital Christian faith. Notably, Yoder adds, this type of renewal offers no distinct challenge to the "established" Church and "tends to remain in the frame of the theocratic society to which it reacts."[31]

In contrast to these two dominant traditions, Yoder suggests that his own tradition, the "Believers' Church," constitutes a third type that offers a way to "move beyond the oscillation between the theocratic and the spiritu-alist patterns."[32] However, it moves beyond these modes not through com-

29. Yoder, "People in the World," 71.
30. Yoder, "People in the World," 71.
31. Yoder, "People in the World," 72.
32. Yoder, "People in the World," 72.

promise or synthesis, but by resisting elements of both the first and second types, namely, the expansion of the Church to a synonymous association with the society (within which all are baptized into the *corpus christianum*) and the reduction of the Church to para-ecclesial forms that nurture the individual's inner or spiritual life. In contrast, the Believer's Church finds its place as a visible community of disciples who distinguish themselves from the whole of society by their shared commitment to a form of life revealed by Jesus and exemplified by the life of the early Church. Yoder argues that it is not theocratic, as it involves only some and not all of the society (emphasizing the "voluntary" nature of the community). Nor is it only a spiritual community, inasmuch as it has a political embodiment; it is an actual body or community of people sharing together in the ecclesiological forms and practices that are "according to scripture and that are expressive of the character of the disciples' fellowship."[33]

In Yoder's typology, the Church's role or place is not questioned by either the theocratic or the spiritualist types. This is so because the center of historical meaning is located in the society or in the spiritual life of the individual; neither considers the Church itself to be the central locus of historical meaning. Yet, Yoder suggests, this is to ignore the witness of the scriptures, which proclaim the "centrality of the Church in God's purposes," namely, to break down walls of division and to raise up a new humanity. As Yoder puts it, "The work of God is the calling of a people, whether in the Old Covenant or the New," and this community constitutes a "new social wholeness . . . which gives meaning to history."[34] In other words, historical meaning finds its place, not in the state or in the inner life of the individual, but rather in the Church, understood specifically as a visible community. In the Believers' Church type, the Church itself is this visible, historical, embodied group of people; thus, Yoder's title for the essay, "A People in the World." This People is the Church.

Yoder seeks to advance a particular argument for the ecclesiological significance of the Believer's Church tradition within the larger ecumenical conversations on the nature and mission of the Church. He portrays John Wesley in the midst of a stream of names and lives that reflect an essential commitment to the importance of what Yoder has broadly called the spiritualist tradition. He writes, "That God is gracious *to me* is the good news that Zinzendorf, Wesley, Kierkegaard, and today both Rudolf Bultmann

33. Yoder, "People in the World," 72.
34. Yoder, "People in the World," 74.

and Billy Graham (in their very different ways) have derived from Luther and have labored to keep unclouded by any effort to derive from it (or to base upon it) a social program or any other human work."[35]

In other words, to leave unchallenged the primacy of God's gratuity in salvation, Yoder argues that these reformers, teachers, preachers, and leaders all made a primary distinction between the work of God in one's individual spiritual life and the consequent formation of "human goals or achievements" that must "be studiously kept in second place."[36] As a result, because each of them has been so formed by the Protestant understanding of individual guilt and subjective forgiveness, each missed what has only come to light due to more recent exegetical work, namely, the biblical witness to the centrality of the Church to God's purposes, the raising up of a particular, reconciled, and reconciling People.

It is instructive to consider Yoder's use of Wesley, inasmuch as it reveals what may be a popular understanding of Wesley and the reform he pursued in the development of the Methodist movement. Specifically, it has been argued that Wesley and Methodism can, even must be, understood primarily as examples of Yoder's spiritualist type, that the focus of the Methodist story can be limited to a particular "heart-warming experience" on Aldersgate Street in 1738, and that from this basis, directions for renewal in the contemporary Church should be taken. Is Yoder's view of Wesley correct?

Supporting Spiritualist and Theocratic Renewal

The answer to this question is "Yes and No." Indeed, while Wesley and the Methodist movement were deeply influenced by the traditions of Continental Pietism, it can be argued that both types of renewal, theocratic and spiritualist, play a part in the developing identity of the Methodist movement. To many, the latter category will seem to fit better than the former because the history of Methodism itself is popularly understood as the history of a *spiritual* renewal movement within an established Church, ostensibly seeking a place for the nurture and exercise of real Christianity within the cold formalism of the larger Church. As mentioned earlier, Wesley was deeply influenced by the Continental reform movements of Moravianism and Pietism, which themselves sought a form of intentional Christian life

35. Yoder, "People in the World," 73.
36. Yoder, "People in the World," 73.

within the larger context of an established Church. It was from these movements that Wesley borrowed the structures that developed into the Methodist movement, specifically the concept of *ecclesiola in ecclesia*.[37]

Remembering the drive in this form of renewal toward addressing the
individual's interior spiritual life, we take particular note of the emphasis in
that definition on the central importance of earnest experience. Were we
to stop here, we might indeed conclude that Wesleyan Methodism fits the
category assigned in Yoder's typology. However, two further considerations
problematize this conclusion and lead us to the broader position that Wesley and the Methodist movement fit not only some descriptive elements of
Yoder's spiritualist type, but also some associated with its theoretical (and
historical) opposite, the theocratic type.

The first consideration is Wesley's fundamental understanding of the
irreplaceable role of the community in the development of the individual's
spiritual life, briefly considered above. Influenced by his anthropology and
moral psychology that placed emphasis on the necessity of ongoing formation of the affections and tempers, Wesley emphasized the importance of
the community that provides accountability in the shaping of the inner and
outer life, both being necessary for a life that could be called holy. Thus,
Wesley clearly believed that, while all must "work out their own salvation,"
none could do so outside of the connection to a community of fellow travelers on the *via salutis*.[38] Location in the faith community was required.[39]

It still might be argued that, even in the community context that is the
ecclesiola, the spiritualist type continues to be descriptively powerful, to the
extent that we are still concerned with renewal of the spiritual (and moral)
lives of individuals. Whether focused on the believer located alone in the
monastic cell or in the context of the gathered congregation, does not the
spiritualist type limit the work of renewal to the spiritual development of
the *inner* life of the individual? We can assume that Wesley would answer
that question in the negative, because it leads us to the second consideration that broadens Wesley's vision of renewal, namely, his postmillennial
eschatological perspective.

While such vision developed over the course of his life, Wesley did
come to believe that the reign of God could not be located solely in the
abstracted, transcendent era to come, but rather appeared in the present

37. Collins, *Theology of John Wesley*, 249. See also Maddox, *Responsible Grace*, 241.

38. See Maddox, *Responsible Grace*; "Wesley's Prescription," 15–28.

39. Wesley, "Sermon on the Mount IV," §1.1, *Works*, 1:533–34.

"through the work of the Spirit in and through believers."[40] As Randy Maddox points out, despite the premillennial influences that appear in earlier years of Wesley's writing, his later sermons reflect themes influential in Puritan circles, specifically the commitment to the postmillennial emphasis on the "silent increase" of God's reign within the created order.[41] This emphasis led Wesley to broaden his concern, not only for the renewal that takes place in the life of the individual believer, but also, and consequently, in the social renewal that these believers would inspire because of their faithful acts in the creation at large.

These eschatological emphases influenced Wesley's understanding of the Church, of the proper location of historical meaning, and thus of the proper focus for renewal. To his preachers, Wesley declared that the mission of the Methodist movement was "not to form any new sect; but to reform the nation, particularly the Church; and to spread scriptural holiness over the land."[42] More particularly, Wesley once argued that the Church "is a body of [people] compacted together in order, first to save each his own soul, then to assist each other in working out their salvation, and afterwards, as far as in them lies, to save all [people] from present and future misery, to overturn the kingdom of Satan, and set up the kingdom of Christ."[43] Thus, it is clear that Wesley did not locate the center of historical meaning solely in the life of the holy individual, but rather, allowed significant room for the consideration of the particular effect such holy individuals would have in relationship to the nation and the world. One precedes and leads to the other. As Maddox puts it, Wesley saw the Church as "a means of social grace—a setting for nurturing Christian character and spawning agents of God's gracious presence in the world."[44] Spiritual renewal led to national renewal.

This connection has fueled the interpretation of Wesley's "functional" understanding of the relationship between soteriological mission and ecclesial order, considered above. The Church is understood to sustain spiritualist renewal in order to foster support for theocratic renewal, as

40. Maddox, *Responsible Grace*, 239.

41. Maddox, *Responsible Grace*, 238–39. It is important to note that, while Yoder associates the "Pietist" movement with his spiritualist type, he associates "Puritans" with the theocratic type. See Yoder, "People in the World," 71n8.

42. Wesley, "Large Minutes," 299.

43. Wesley, "Reformation of Manners," §2, *Works*, 2:302.

44. Maddox, *Responsible Grace*, 135. Maddox locates a consideration of Wesley's ecclesiology directly following a treatment of Wesley's postmillennialism.

holy believers who love God will inevitably turn to love their neighbor(s). As a result, it is too simple to say that Wesley is merely a Pietist spiritualist, just as it is too much to say that he is solely concerned with reform of the society or the nation, the realm of concern for Yoder's theocrat. Wesley is concerned with both spiritual renewal and national renewal, the one hopefully leading to the other.

Problematizing Spiritualist and Theocratic Renewal

While this recognition might help us overcome the limitations of Yoder's description of Wesley and his Methodist movement, it does not help us overcome the limitations Yoder identifies at work in both forms of renewal. He argues that each of these forms of renewal resists the other to the extent that each represents a center of historical meaning that can be plotted on opposite ends of a continuum, one end representing the inner life of the individual, and the other the society as a whole. Thus, to seek to bring spiritualist and theocratic positions into one another's orbit can only result (and has resulted) in confusions in defining the identity and mission of the Church. This fundamental incompatibility leads to the oscillations between these polarities which, Yoder argues, describes much of the conversation in the modern ecumenical movement.

This, however, has not stopped efforts to bridge these differences. In fact, we can draw on Yoder's reference to the fact that, when one focuses on the issue of ethics or holy living from both perspectives, spiritualism and theocracy "are more alike than different, for the concentration on personal authenticity and on social control is not contradictory but complementary."[45] This is because the converted individual who embodies the virtues of humility and servitude is most properly equipped for faithful and effective service in the roles given in the so-called secular state. Consequently, these two positions actually need one another. Spiritualists are drawn out of their sequestered settlement in the inward reaches of the individual soul and into the vital work of the real world to which they bring the fruit of a spiritual life and the zeal that only the truly converted can display.

Even so, given the fundamental difference in the location of historical meaning of these two types, Yoder argues that, while the spiritualist may recognize the importance of social action, this does not necessarily require the relocation of historical meaning from its placement in the spiritual

45. Yoder, "People in the World," 79.

renewal of each individual believer. The same issue applies when we begin from the other side of the spectrum. So, although the theocrat might understand the necessity of radical commitment or even conversion for the sustaining of agents in their work for social change, it remains the case that the location of historical meaning resides in the belief that "what ultimately matters in God's purpose is the building of better society."[46] What Yoder leads us to see is the futility of being stuck in endless and hopeless argument over which pole on the spectrum of renewal represents the greater faithfulness. The result, he suggests, is an oscillation between poles that should seem familiar to students of ecclesiastical history and to those engaged in contemporary ecumenical and intra-denominational arguments between those who prefer evangelism or social justice.[47]

This impasse leads Yoder to a third option, the location in which God has already chosen to carry historical meaning, namely, "a People in the world." He says, "I shall claim that the Church is called to move beyond the oscillation between the theocratic and the spiritualist patterns, not to a compromise between the two or to a synthesis claiming like Hegel to 'assume' them both, but to what is genuinely a third option,"[48] the Believer's Church.

Considering Wesley's postmillennial concern for renewal of holiness in the spirit and in the nation, we are led to ask if Wesley and early Methodism reflect, to some extent, threads of both traditions of renewal that we are calling spiritualist and theocratic. Does this mean that Methodism was, and is, consigned to the endless oscillation between types of renewal and their differing locations of historical meaning? Is Methodism located on shaky ecclesiological ground that ignores the central influence of Yoder's third type?

While both streams of tradition (the "spiritualist" and the "theocratic") may be said to be present in Wesley and in early Methodism, neither of them can stand, on their own or as woven together, as proper descriptions of the entirety of Methodist identity and mission. We now turn to a consideration of Wesley and the early Methodist movement to show that, while Methodism was a movement that sought renewal of the Spirit and the Nation, it only did so as a "People in the World."

46. Yoder, "People in the World," 91.

47. Yoder, "People in the World," 90–91.

48. Yoder, "People in the World," 72–73.

Wesley, the General Rules, and the Development of Methodist Peoplehood

L. Gregory Jones and Michael Cartwright suggested that "one of the primary factors enabling the 'people *called* Methodist' to become the '*people called* Methodist' in early Methodism was the practice of the General Rules through the class meetings and gatherings of the societies."[49] Taking their lead, I hope to show how the General Rules accomplished this formation by reflecting three areas where Wesley placed particular emphasis when considering the ecclesiological shape of the early Methodist movement: first, on the *Visibility* of the embodied, gathered community; second, on the *Practices* that shape the inner life of the Methodist Societies; and third, on the *Witness* that this community offers to those outside in the world.

Visibility of Embodied Community

First, the Rules describe the common life of a *visible* People. Wesley's account of the General Rules begins not with any abstracted vision of what a community *might* be, but rather, he begins with a historical account: "Eight or ten persons came to me in London who appeared to be deeply convinced of sin, and earnestly groaning for redemption. . . . I appointed a day when they might all come together, which from thenceforward they did every week. . . . This was the rise of the United Society."[50]

Methodism cannot be understood apart from the historical reality of a gathered community of people seeking the holiness that the General Rules were developed to create and nurture. Behind this reality is not only Wesley's understanding of the visibility of the Church, but also his commitment to the irreducible identity of Christianity as a "social religion" that "cannot subsist at all without society, without living and conversing with other [people]."[51] This communal emphasis problematizes any attempt to render Wesley or early Methodism as pure examples of Yoder's spiritualist type. While there is a focus on the formation of holiness in the life of each believer, and while each is encouraged to "work out your own salvation," there is no question that this cannot be an individualistic endeavor. Embodiment in community is required.

49. Jones and Cartwright, "Vital Congregations," 96n22.
50. Wesley, "General Rules," §1–2, *Works*, 9:69.
51. Wesley, "Sermon on the Mount IV," §1.1, *Works*, 1:533–34.

Of course, one reason this People called Methodist was visible was due to the contrast it created against the backdrop of the lack of visible Christian belief and practice in the larger established Church. In some sense, this is why most of Wesley's writing about ecclesiology tended to be in the form of response to critics who claimed that in Methodism, Wesley intended a separation from the Church of England.

Practices That Shape the Inner Life

The visibility of the People lay in the work of and ways of life that defined this community as a particular People called Methodist. We see Wesley's commitment to the necessity of such practices in the visible, gathered community of faith in his well-known response to a critic:

> If it be said, "But there are some true Christians in the parish, and you destroy the Christian fellowship between these and them," I answer: That which never existed cannot be destroyed. But the fellowship you speak of never existed. Therefore it cannot be destroyed. Which of those true Christians had any such fellowship with these? Who watched over them in love? Who marked their growth in grace? Who advised and exhorted them from time to time? Who prayed with them and for them as they had need? This, and this alone, is Christian fellowship. . . . The real truth is just the reverse of this: we introduce Christian fellowship where it was utterly destroyed. And the fruits of it have been peace, joy, love, and zeal for every good word and work.[52]

Against invisibility, disembodiment, and the inconsequential ties that render the Church a gathering of people no stronger than "a mere rope of sand," Wesley argues for the necessity of common discipline and accountability in an actual gathering of people in order for there to be a community present that can bear the name Christian. Once again, in defending his movement, we hear Wesley arguing for a robust vision of a particular People who are made visible as they share in a particular form of life together.[53]

52. Wesley, "Plain Account," §1.11, *Works*, 9:258–59.

53. See Wesley's sermon, "On Schism," which is also a sermon from the "Late Wesley," in which Wesley makes a clear judgment about the relationship of "nominal" Christians to the Church. Considering the issue of schism and division in the body of the Church, Wesley writes, "This indeed is not of so much consequence to *you* who are only a *nominal* Christian. For you are not now vitally united to any of the members of Christ. *Though you are called a Christian you are not really a member of any Christian Church*" (Wesley,

This emphasis continues in the "Late Wesley." Even in Wesley's nearly last word on ecclesiology, the previously considered sermon "Of the Church," Wesley turns from encouraging a wide berth in understanding the Church's catholicity and toward a clear argument for understanding the holiness of the Church, called to "walk worthy of the vocation wherewith we are called."[54] Such walking is "to think, speak, and act, in every instance in a manner worthy of our Christian calling."[55] This leads to discussion about the spiritual formation necessary that will shape lives capable of living in such a manner, and concludes with a clear call for the necessity of such formation taking place within the context of the community that lives and practices this life together.

This concern for formation should affect the way we read the General Rules and conceive of their function and purpose in the Methodist movement. It is clear enough that the Rules are structured in such a way as to encourage the formation of holiness in the Methodist gatherings to which they gave shape and guidance. Under each of the three rules, Wesley is able to spell out in clear terms the particular adhesions and renunciations that constitute evidence of the "desire of salvation" and that reflect "walking worthily." Because the requirements to join a class meeting in early Methodism were so minimal—only the desire for salvation was necessary—the General Rules supplied the "basics for Christian living in the world with whatever 'degree of faith' one had been graced."[56]

The Rules, therefore, can be seen to have fulfilled a catechetical function, introducing the ways of discipleship, the specific patterns of the way of a Christian in the world. From these very social, communal practices of piety and mercy, the disciple "confidently expected the blessings of God's grace, first to bring [her] the assurance of faith, and then to build [her] up as [an] obedient [disciple]."[57] Thus, resisting any tendency in the contemporary Church to understand Methodist faith as solely an experience of the inward assurance of saving faith that precedes the engagement with the life and practices of the community, Lowes Watson argues strongly for

---

"On Schism," §2.18, *Works*, 3:68). Can we extrapolate from here that to be part of the Church for Wesley, one must participate in the vital community produced by the fusion of practices and structures detailed in the General Rules?

54. Wesley, "Of the Church," §2.20, *Works*, 3:53.

55. Wesley, "Of the Church," §2.20, *Works*, 3:53.

56. Watson, "Class Leaders and Class Meetings," 245–64; "Aldersgate Street," 33–47.

57. Watson, "Aldersgate Street," 45–46.

the necessary engagement with the very particular practices among People called Methodist as integral to salvation. Here we must remember Yoder's point that it is from the perspective of this particular community that both "personal conversion (whereby individuals are called into this meaning) and missionary instrumentalities are derived."[58] Drawing from the first half of that sentence, we can see that the spiritual renewal of the individual is defined here by the central importance of the visible community and its shared practices, without which evangelism and conversion become unintelligible.

Witness Made Evident in the World

The fact that "missionary instrumentalities" are also shaped by their primary location inside the community of faith guides us to the consideration of Wesley's *third* emphasis. The visible and practicing People called Methodist are sent in mission and witness to the world. Wesley closes his sermon, "Of the Church," with encouragement directed to this holy People in language that displays both the necessary visibility of the Church as well as a vision of the Church in eschatological terms that serve as a particular witness to the world. "In the meantime," Wesley writes, between now and the coming of the Kingdom,

> let all those who are real members of the Church see that they walk holy and unblameable in all things. . . . Show [all] your faith by your works. Let them see by the whole tenor of your conversation that your hope is all laid up above! Let all your words and actions evidence the spirit whereby you are animated! Above all things, let your love abound. Let it extend to every child of man; let it overflow to every child of God. By this let all men [sic] know whose disciples ye are, because you love one another.[59]

Wesley makes a distinction here between the Church and the "men [sic] of the world" and the "lover(s) of the world" who are guided by different commitments and who are "dead to God." The "real members of the

---

58. Yoder, "People in the World," 74.

59. Wesley, "Of the Church," §3.30, *Works*, 3:56–57. See also Wesley's sermon, "Sermon on the Mount IV," particularly §2.2, where we have seen that Wesley makes clear that Christianity requires community, but where he also goes on to suggest that, when "real" among believers, it cannot be hidden from the watching world.

Church" are called to a different way, not just in belief, but in "words and actions," embodied and visible, on display to the world.[60]

Such words and actions find clear and detailed expression in the General Rules, where Wesley describes very specific spiritual, bodily, economic, and community practices that are required of Methodists. However, rather than just reading these rules as the encouragements to individuals continuing in the Society, we must note how they also reflect Wesley's understanding of the relationship of Church and world, and how the adherence to the injunction to do no harm and to do "good of every possible sort and as far as is possible to all men" has a cost for those within this community of witness. To live in this way, Wesley suggests, means that Methodists must also seek to do good

> by running with patience the race that is set before them; "denying themselves, and taking up their cross daily"; submitting to bear the reproach of Christ, to be as the filth and offscouring of the world; and looking that men [sic] should "say all manner of evil of them falsely, for their Lord's sake."[61]

The holiness of the Church is discovered in the holiness of its members, and together, in the practices and ways of their common holy lives, they render the Church visible in the world, perhaps to be rejected by the world, but sent to witness to that world all the same. As Wesley put it,

> We look upon the Methodists (so called) in general, not as any particular party; (this would exceedingly obstruct the grand design, for which we conceive God has raised them up), but as living witnesses, in and to every party, of that Christianity which we preach; which is hereby demonstrated to be a real thing, and visibly held out to all the world.[62]

In these three emphases, particularly reflected in the General Rules, Wesley named the conditions necessary to create and sustain a particular People, defined by its visibility, formed and sustained by its practices, and sent to the world as a witness to God's creating and reconciling work. When we keep in mind this Peoplehood that Wesley encouraged and formed in his early Methodist movement through the General Rules, we see connections to Yoder's third type, identified as the location of historical meaning

---

60. Wesley, "Of the Church," §3.28, 29, *Works*, 3:56.

61. Wesley, "General Rules," §5, *Works*, 9:72.

62. Wesley, "Reasons Against a Separation," §3.1, *Works*, 9:337.

and renewal discovered in the Believer's Church tradition. Philip Meadows suggests:

> This Anabaptist thinking [regarding the Church as a social reality] tempts me to take liberty with the meaning of early Methodist "societies." *Each society, bound by a common rule and a set of common practices could easily be thought of as a "social reality" in its own right.* Their public, cultural and political life was that of striving after scriptural holiness. The "General Rule" (of doing no harm, doing all the good they can, and attending to the means of grace) had the effect of holding them to a form of Kingdom living that resisted selfish ambition and accumulation in favour of good stewardship. . . . And he guides them in the use of money to earn all they can (i.e., without injury to self or neighbour), save all they can (i.e., not wasting what they have earned), and give all they can (i.e., of that which exceeds their own basic needs). Wesley aims to describe a way of life literally consistent with the language of the Ten Commandments and the teaching of Jesus found in the Sermon on the Mount (a text much used by Anabaptists). I am again indebted to the Anabaptists for helping me see how a Christian community that embodies the gospel does not happen by accident, but requires an intentional commitment to a form of life capable of resisting the dominant social realities of the world.[63]

I argue that this connection between the societies that comprised the early Methodist movement, created and guided by the General Rules and their identification as ecclesial entities in their own right, is not at all farfetched.

Given Wesley's own commitments to a Methodist Peoplehood defined by its visibility, holy practices, and witness to the world, Meadows's connection may be more than an interesting idea, reflective of Wesley's manifestation of the influence from the Believer's Church tradition. Consequently, each of the societies in the early Methodist movement should be understood as a People in the World, each, as Meadows suggests, a social reality in its own right.[64] To fully understand the meaning of the Methodist renewal, then, we must take Yoder's typology very seriously, and admit that beyond spiritualist or theocratic interests, Wesleyan Methodism began as a movement to develop a visible, practicing, and witnessing holy People called Methodists. If this is the case, then the understanding of early

---

63. Meadows, "Anabaptist Leanings" (emphasis mine).

64. Meadows, "Anabaptist Leanings."

Methodism as a movement for spiritualist or theocratic renewal faces a challenge, as both types of renewal must now first be located in and shaped by the primary identity of the Methodist Peoplehood.

I believe this is what Wesley envisioned when he offered up the General Rules: not only a renewal movement within the larger Church, but a community of holy People who make up a visible community, practicing discipleship in the means of grace and witnessing to the world. Thus, against interpretations of Wesleyan Methodism as a purely spiritualist or pietistic movement, and also against interpretations that place its sole focus on the reform of the nation, we must conclude that Wesley's own hopes for renewal in the Church and the nation could not be separated from their location within the visible, disciplined, and witnessing *People* called Methodist.

Implications for (United Methodist) Ecclesiology and Evangelistic Mission

This sense of a Methodist Peoplehood should play a more significant role in contemporary conversations about Methodist ecclesial identity, mission, and practice. While a reincarnation of early Methodist life cannot be the goal here, reflection on the People called Methodist can provide contemporary Methodism with historical memory that has the potential to interrogate current assumptions and beliefs regarding the nature of the Church, its mission, and the potential sources for renewal.

It is beyond the limits of this chapter to consider the complex historical account of the development of Methodism not only in Britain, but also, and more particularly, in America, where the movement first became a Church.[65] However, what we can confidently say is that Yoder's named oscillation between spiritualist and theocratic polarities has been with us for some time. As Randy Maddox reminds us,

---

65. In fact, while this chapter will not enter into the historical account of the developing role the General Rules played in later, post-Wesleyan British and American Methodism, it is particularly vital to understand their defining influence in early American Methodism. As Randy Maddox states, "the operative definition of 'Church' in early American Methodism was that of the society in the *General Rules.*" It is equally important to understand the loss of the *Rules* in that same context. For excellent accounts of the General Rules' function and their loss in the American context, see Maddox, "Social Grace," 131–60; Jones and Cartwright, "Vital Congregations," 97–110.

North American Protestantism of the early twentieth century tended to divide across the board into warring camps over the mission of the Church. The result was all-too-often a lamentable polarization between concern for the spiritual transformation of individual lives and efforts for the socio-economic transformation of an alienating and oppressive social order. This polarization was as frequent in Methodist circles as anywhere else, and its after-shocks remain with us.[66]

One place I believe this division is evident is in the contemporary treatment of the General Rules in the discipline and life of the contemporary UMC.

Until they lost their place, the General Rules had a defining position in the ecclesiological identity of the early American Methodist Church.[67] Their loss, however, was such that today they have been relatively unknown in The United Methodist Church, relegated to a section in the *Book of Discipline* rarely visited and often eclipsed by the more familiar *Social Principles*.[68] Greater awareness of the *Rules* did follow when they were slightly redeveloped by Bishop Ruben P. Job and released as *Three Simple Rules: A Wesleyan Way of Living*." Even so, I fear the adaptation had the (perhaps unintended) effect of removing the *Rules* from their location in the tradition and in the communal life of the Methodist "People" that I seek to describe in this chapter. Job redevelops Wesley's third rule, suggesting "Stay in love with God" as a replacement for Wesley's language, originally calling the People called Methodist to "[attend] upon all the ordinances of God."[69] While Job clearly understood the significance of Christian practices, or "means of grace" in the formation of holiness, his rephrasing may have led some to lose the clear connection Wesley's third rule makes

---

66. Maddox, "Social Grace," 148. Maddox points readers to Schmidt's *Souls or the Social Order* as a "pioneering study of this development" (148n117).

67. "Under the influence of the 'social gospel,' the 'Social Creed' (1908, 1952) would complete the process of supplanting the '*General Rules*' as a primary focus of moral discipline for 'the people called Methodist.' By the time the 1972 *Book of Discipline of the United Methodist Church* is published, the 'Social Principles' have taken center stage, and the 'General Rules of the United Societies' have been placed in a section called 'Foundation Documents'" (Jones and Cartwright, "Vital Congregations," 107).

68. The Social Principles are Part V of United Methodist Church, *Book of Discipline 2016*, para. 160–66, 105–46. "The General Rules of the Methodist Church" are found in United Methodist Church, *Book of Discipline 2016*, para. 104, 77–80, which is located within Part III, "Doctrinal Standards and Our Theological Task," para. 102–5, 47–91.

69. Job, *Three Simple Rules*, 53.

between traditioned practices of Christian formation and the development of Christian discipleship. Of greater concern is the possibility that some read Job's adaptation of the rules as a source for personal or individual devotion, dislocating the *Rules* from their communal setting, shaping not just holy people, but a holy "People" called Methodist.

With this treatment the *Social Principles* appear to be the resource to address contemporary issues, while the General Rules have come to be identified as a resource to shape the inward spiritual life of the believer. In short, here we see the differentiation between spiritualist and theocratic orientations operating to place these documents in such a way as to suggest that contemporary Methodism cannot simply choose one over the other, spirituality or social responsibility, but instead must seek to embody both.

Yet, according to Yoder, this is a reconciliation that cannot be brokered if we allow that the differences between spirituality and social responsibility, between evangelism and social justice, between spiritualist and theocratic renewal, are differences in locations of historical meaning. If this is granted, then what becomes necessary is a third option, and as we have seen, Yoder offers us the Believer's Church tradition, locating historical meaning in the People of God. God created this particular People from Abraham, liberated them from Egypt, called them together as the Body of Christ, and also, as I have sought to show in this study, formed them from the parishes of eighteenth-century England to be the People called Methodist. What I am suggesting, therefore, is the necessary inclusion of Peoplehood as a vital element of Methodist ecclesial identity and evangelistic mission. One place this inclusion is evident is the General Rules. When we speak about the People called Methodist in these ways, we will find the resources we need to go beyond the oscillation and argumentation over the proper center for Methodist identity and renewal, and will find a location that will render intelligible for contemporary purposes Wesley's postmillennial hope for the transformation of lives and the world.

Against this conclusion, one might argue that it must be acknowledged that David Lowes Watson was right that the significant difference between the ecclesiological status of the contemporary UMC versus that of the early Methodist societies makes a direct importation of the General Rules and the formation of a distinct Methodist peoplehood quite impossible.[70] In essence, the argument goes, we cannot reasonably expect the rigorous discipline of early Methodism to find a happy home in the

70. Watson, "Aldersgate Street," 46.

contemporary congregations that constitute United Methodism—an argument that is, most likely, quite correct. In response, however, one might first offer a counter-concern, namely, that such warnings tend to allow the continuation of what has developed into a generalized amnesia regarding the central importance (and eventual marginalization) of the General Rules in the story of Methodism and, consequently, a dismissal of the *Rules* as containing any meaningful guidance for the shape of contemporary Methodist life. Even so, contemporary Methodism cannot be exonerated from the responsibility to pay attention to the *Rules*, to the form of community they created, and to the ways in which they might guide contemporary ecclesiological conversation.

Of course, the primary reason to suggest the adoption of the notion of Peoplehood of the Church is for the sake of articulating a theology of evangelism for Methodism that truly leans both ways at once. Envisioning the Church as a People is a move toward resisting the understatement of the Church/World difference in ways that lead to the eventual collapse of the former into the latter. As discussed in the second chapter, given the formative agency of the principalities and the powers, particularly those in service to the ends of the modern market, focus on the Church as a People is critical. Under the conditions of life in what Philip Bobbitt has called the "market-state," rendering all citizens therein primarily as consumers, how can the Church be perceived as anything other than a provider of goods and services, competing for the most significant resources consumers have to give, namely, their money and their time?[71] Despite any awareness inside the Church that it lives within the context of the "market-state," and regardless of any efforts made from within the Church to resist and subvert such a categorization, the formative power of the market-state cannot be denied; even the Church that consciously seeks to live as a counter-cultural community, located off the grid, can still be (and often is) readily adopted as yet another product offered to fulfill the needs of yet another demographically identified niche within the market population. Furthermore, such conditions have a negative effect on the actual visibility of the Church, inasmuch

71. Rowan Williams writes, "[Bobbitt] sees our present context as one where the nation state's inability to deliver in the terms we have become used to, its inability to meet the expectations we now bring, has led to a shift into a new political mode, the market state, in which the function of government—and the thing that makes government worth obeying—is to clear a space for individuals or groups to do their own negotiating, to secure the best deal or the best value for money in pursuing what they want" (Williams, "Richard Dimbleby Lecture," para. 11).

as the world is watching only that which it is formed to watch, namely, that which rises to the level of visibility through forms of specified advertising shaped by the demographic knowledge of the end user. Consequently, as Stone acknowledges, it may be the case that the Church's practices, when actually made visible to a watching world, will surely be misconstrued, judged as odd, or actually dismissed by the world. However, without the density of the historical community, the Peoplehood of the Church as visible, practicing, and witnessing, the possibility for evangelistic witness grows weak.

Thus, I want to further encourage the renewed focus on the General Rules, as both United Methodist doctrine and as a key source for the development of a Methodist sense of Peoplehood, and to connect the General Rules as United Methodist Doctrine to the practical theological task of developing local expressions with concern for both traditional consistency and practical wisdom. There are three potential leanings or directions for such conversations.

First, these reflections draw attention to the congregation. Rather than seeking to balance ministries of spiritual renewal and evangelism with ministries of mission and social witness, a focus on the Peoplehood formed and sustained in the *Rules* emphasizes the nature of the congregation itself. In that context, a key element of practical, pastoral theological leadership seeking the contemporary contextualization of the General Rules will be to facilitate questions such as: "What are the practices of holy living and the means of grace among us today, and which have we forgotten over time?" And, "How is our life together as a People a witness to the world, a 'sign, sacrament, and herald of God's presence and God's reign'"?[72] Small steps like these may help to broaden the ecclesial imagination, to re-vision the congregation as a particular People in the world, and to reclaim the formative importance of the General Rules.

Second, I suggest that these emphases also draw us to look to broader conversations for potential overlap and mutual enrichment. Other signs of renewal appear in contemporary movements that have sought to reclaim the role of the common rule within disciplined communities, movements to which we should pay close attention and seek to engage in ongoing conversation. For example, we have much to learn from the ongoing conversations

---

72. Kenneson suggests that the Church is the "embodied presence" of "visible grace," and as such, the Church is sent to the world as the "sign, sacrament, and herald of God's presence and God's reign" (Kenneson, "Visible Grace," 169–79).

in the development of the "New Monasticism" within communities that emulate the fusion of spiritual and social concern from within a distinct, rule-based community.[73] Elaine Heath and Scott Kisker's *Longing for Spring: A New Vision for Wesleyan Community* makes these connections more explicitly.[74]

These reflections push toward a third context for more conversation: increased interest in new congregational development or Church planting. The United Methodist Church has sustained over several years the "Path One" initiative to plant new congregations. However, in light of such missional commitments, we must ask what theological, and more specifically, ecclesiological, imagination shapes such work. When we seek to plant new churches, are the visions for these communities of faith influenced at all by the vision of a People created and nurtured by the communal practice of the General Rules? Here again, a more focused reflection on Methodist Peoplehood raises questions about the shape of new ecclesial community: are such communities formed to resemble the megachurch, the monastery, the non-profit social service agency, or something that leans both ways at once? Further reflections on the implications of a Methodist ecclesial identity defined in the terms of "Peoplehood" will continue in the next chapter as we turn to consider the shape of the Church's agency in evangelism.

Conclusion

In an attempt to make the first constructive move in a Methodist ecclesiology and theology of evangelistic mission, I have asserted that Methodism is a People, and that such a designation informs Methodist ecclesial identity. We should think of the Church as more than the context or environment housing the practices pursuing soteriological mission. Through "social grace" active in a community following Wesley's General Rules, what formed was a visible, practicing, and witnessing People called Methodist.

This chapter, then, has intentionally leaned just one way: into the history, theology, and practices that form a People called Methodist. In the desire to articulate a theology of evangelism resistant to the understatement of the Church/World difference, the concern for the identity and practices that render the Church a visible, practicing, and witnessing community are crucial. Yet, it is not enough to lean just one way.

73. Rutba House, *School(s) for Conversion.*
74. Heath and Kisker, *Longing for Spring.*

In the next chapter I will complicate the theological identity of a Methodist People as we turn to consider the Church's agency in the practice of evangelism. In this frame, such a People are constantly appearing in the Church's ongoing missional-evangelistic engagement with the world. Again, my hope is to build on Stone's gesture toward this location of the Church, by suggesting not only this Church's visual, aesthetic witness to the world, but also its direct, embodied engagement with the world. Further, I will seek to articulate how this construction opens us to a reading of Methodism that relates this sense of Peoplehood to connectional identity, and to the Church's presence in the congregation, and also beyond the congregation, in the innovative development of organizations and institutions that embody and extend the Church's presence in the world. In other words, we must now complicate our vision and seek an account of the Church and its missional-evangelistic practice that really does lean both ways at once.

4

Intercessory Evangelism

It seems that the calling of the laity is above all to intercede. To be an advocate within the world for the powerless and victims is inseparable from the task of representing the powerless before God. Where I stand, day by day in the world, will determine what I can and must do in the liturgy where the connections of the world and the Kingdom are woven afresh.[1]

Introduction

IN THE LAST CHAPTER, I located Methodist ecclesial identity in the formation of a "People," a community formed from the practices embedded in Wesley's General Rules, devotion to which led to the development of a visible, practicing, and witnessing People called Methodist. This constituted a step toward articulating the stance the Church takes in a theology of evangelistic mission: the Church is a "People in the world."

Yet, this identification of the People called Methodist was only one step in a study that seeks to elucidate a theology of evangelism that leans both ways at once. The recognition of the visible, practicing, witnessing identity of the People called Methodist is critical to a theology of evangelism that maintains the differentiation of Church/World. But on its own, it is incomplete, as our account of ecclesial formation still requires the critical connection to an account of evangelistic mission, articulated in consideration of

1. Williams, "Being a People," 16.

the Church's agency. In other words, Methodism might constitute a People in the world, but now we must ask: how does this People *engage* the world?

Answering this question will require us to complicate the theological identity of a Methodist People. In this chapter, I will argue that a Methodist People is not only shaped in the practice of the General Rules, but also, at the same time, in the ongoing evangelistic engagement with the world. Put differently, a Methodist Peoplehood is constantly "appearing" and is "discovered" as it takes shape at the intersection of the Church and the world. Further, I will suggest that the shape of that engagement is a sense of evangelism best described and embodied as "intercession." Intercession describes the agency of the People called Methodist standing at the intersection of God and the world, fully embodied as the Church, and fully present and engaged as the Church in the world, leaning both ways at once. Finally, I will articulate how this image of an emerging People in the world opens us to the connection between this sense of Peoplehood and Methodist connectional identity, and more particularly, to the Church's presence beyond the congregation. The People called Methodist engage the world in evangelistic mission in the local Church, to be sure, but also beyond the congregation, in Conference and Connection, as well as in the formation of communities that are themselves means of grace, embodied in the shape of schools, (so-called) non-profit organizations, "Fresh Expressions," Christian social innovations, and neo-monastic ecclesial communities. With this broader imagination regarding the embodiment of the People called Methodist, I offer a vision of Methodist ecclesial identity for the sake of evangelistic mission within the differentiation of Church/World, a People identified by their leaning both ways at once.

Complicating Peoplehood amidst Church and World

I have sought to articulate Peoplehood as a key aspect of Methodist ecclesial identity. Methodism is a People, but such a People must be understood to be embodied in a variety of movements, organizations, and institutions, the relationships between which are governed by an identity Methodists call connectionalism. Given this complexity, we ask in what ways do these instantiations of Methodist presence continue the presence of the Church in the world?

Here the theological vision of Rowan Williams is useful, for Williams is uncomfortable with the overly determinative separation of Church/

World, but not to the degree that he is willing to abandon an account of the evangelistic engagement between the two. On the one hand, he resists the triumphalism endemic to a Church that lives in unquestioned relationship with the political and economic powers and principalities of modern states and markets. Yet, equally important is the fact that Williams does not retreat from the establishment of the Church, nor from the concomitant responsibility to inhabit that space and to speak to the world(s) of politics, economics, culture, and art—as he has done in so many of his works. In navigating these relationships, Williams shows himself to be a theologian who lives within the dialectical complexity of life in the Church/World. In this way, he speaks to the Church as it pursues its evangelistic mission in the world, inasmuch as he attends to what it means to lean both ways at once.

Rather than positing a clear set of ecclesial marks that might be utilized to describe only a materially locatable Church, Williams's vision destabilizes the effort to identify the spatially oriented ontology of the Church, and allows for a more fluid, less "territorial" approach. Inasmuch as this vision impacts his understanding of Church/World, it also affects his understanding of the missional relationship between them. The evangelistic mission of the Church, then, can only be the constant movement of the Church from the memory of its past to the interrogation of its present, and from repentance of its sin to the world of "division and competition" within which the offer of the unrestricted communion of the Trinitarian life reflected and enacted in Jesus can be heard as *good news*. Thus, Williams can be used as a resource to express the theological differentiation of Church/World and the meaning of missional engagement without obviating the true "messiness" of life simultaneously lived in Church/World, or overstating a pristine ontological, "territorial" status for the Church.

The Inescapability of the World

One imagines that the former Archbishop of Canterbury does not think of the Church as entirely separable from the world; from a position of authority within an established Church such overstated separation can hardly be an imaginable reality. Yet, it also cannot be assumed that Williams believes the Church to be faithful when it lives unquestioningly within its establishment. Instead, as he makes clear in his introduction to the essays in *On Christian Theology,* Williams's theological approach, inasmuch as it always assumes that its work begins "in the middle of things," is constantly operating in the unstable, ambiguous space between the Church and the world.[2] It is, in fact, difficult to find much explicit reflection in Williams's work on the *distinction* or the *differentiation* of the Church and the world. Rather, he speaks of their relationship as *angular* or *parabolic*,[3] suggesting that the Church exists as a community "at an angle to the forms of human association we treat as natural," not disconnected from those forms of life, but simultaneously connected, and yet still differentiated, entering the relationship from a different direction, and yet, still as a "context which relativizes all others."[4]

Williams thus maps out a space between Church/World that cannot be inhabited without some tension, in a "paradox [that] is a hard one to live out."[5] On the one hand, the Church must exist in some sense as a sectarian body, a particular People, for

> if we are to keep on learning about Christ, then at the very least the Church needs practices, conventions and life-patterns that keep alive the distinctiveness of the Body. . . . To use the heavily loaded language common in these discussions; a church which does not at least possess certain features of a "sect" cannot act as an agent of transformation.[6]

2. Williams argues that theology is at once "communicative" and "critical" (as well as "celebratory" throughout), which is to say that it is attentive to cultural, linguistic practices both inside and outside the Church. The communicative dynamic leads theology to seek "experiment[ation] with the rhetoric of its uncommitted environment," believing that such an interaction can (and more confidently, will) lead to the expression of the Gospel in ways that are both new and faithful. However, the achievement of faithfulness in this communicative endeavor is gained through theology's attention to critical discourse—the "nagging at fundamental meanings" that keeps theology faithful to its source across time. To call all of this "celebratory" clarifies that for Williams, the focus for this work is not only theological discourse within the academy, but rather, within the Church, and even more specifically, for the achievement of faithful practice of worship and prayer. See Williams, *On Christian Theology*, xii.

3. "Theology should be equipping us for the recognition of and response to the parabolic in the world—all that resists the control of capital and administration and hints at or struggles to a true sharing of human understanding, in art, science and politics. It should also equip us to act parabolically as Christians, to construct in our imagining and our acting 'texts' about conversion—not translations of doctrines into digestible forms, but effective images of a new world like the parables of Christ" (Williams, *On Christian Theology*, 42).

4. Williams, *On Christian Theology*, 233.

5. Williams, *On Christian Theology*, 233.

6. Williams, *On Christian Theology*, 233.

However, this does not mean, in any sense, that the Church must take on all features of a "sect," and thus seek to overstate the material distance between it and the world. To do this would be a mistake, Williams argues, inasmuch as such a move treats "people as if they were not deeply and permanently moulded by their natural and unchosen belonging, to a family or a language group or a political system."[7] Such an assumption is "manifestly damaging and illusory," as "the persons who are involved in the community of the Kingdom are not 'new creations' in the sense of having all their relationships and affiliations cancelled."[8] Rather, we always begin where we are, and with what we have: languages, cultures, practices, relationships, and so on. As created, we are part of creation; we are in the world. Thus, the search for such a space separated from the multiple and overlapping communities that constitute our social lives is a search for something that does not exist, because we always begin "in the middle of things." And so, as a result, Williams suggests,

> The question thus becomes how existing patterns of belonging can collaborate with the patterns of new community, if at all, how the goals and priorities of these existing patterns are to be brought together with the constructive work of the Kingdom, the Body.[9]

In other words, he asks how we can navigate Christian existence between Church/World, leaning both ways at once.

Here, we can begin to see themes which come to bear on the development of a faithful Methodist account of the Church's agency in evangelistic mission. Because the Church is not the world but is sent to participate in divine mission to and within the world, and because the Church is thus always located in the world "in the middle of things," the paradoxical stance that the Church's evangelistic witness takes calls for acts of discernment and proclamation that may take the form of potential cooperation between the Church and elements of the world. As Williams writes,

> The work continues, for the theologian and the Church at large, of discerning and naming the Christ-like events of liberation and humanization in the world *as* Christ-like, and, at the level of action,

---

7. Williams, *On Christian Theology*, 235–36.

8. Williams, *On Christian Theology*, 235–36.

9. Williams, *On Christian Theology*, 236.

expressing this hermeneutical engagement in terms of concrete practical solidarity.[10]

The Church's interpretive work may lead to opportunities for tactical alliances, or in Williams's terms, "concrete practical solidarity." Conversely, such naming may lead to explicit renunciation, which itself constitutes a missional expression of public witness. My point is that all of this becomes unintelligible without an account of the distinction of the Church and the world. The interpretive discernment of the world is the work of a People in the world and is crucial for the account of ecclesial evangelism developing here.

But it is here that Williams troubles these categories as I have deployed them so far. Williams suggests that discernment describes not only the practice of determining potential collaborative efforts between Church/World, but also the determination of the Church itself. In other words, the Church's density and visibility is discovered not upon reflection on its relationship with the wider world, but rather, when and as the Church is engaged in and with the world. In Williams, this move appears in the process of eschewing overly fixed terms to describe the Church's identity and agency. Rather than positing a clear set of ecclesial marks that might be utilized to describe a materially locatable Church, Williams's vision destabilizes the effort to identify the spatially oriented ontology of the Church and allows for a much more fluid, less territorial approach. Inasmuch as this vision impacts his understanding of Church/World, it also affects his understanding of the missional relationship between them. In this way, Williams places any sense of an overly fixed ecclesiology in check.

In "The Judgment of the World," Williams critiques the intratextual project of George Lindbeck's *The Nature of Doctrine*. He argues that Lindbeck's offering constitutes an overdetermination of the relationship between scripture and world, inasmuch as it treats each of these categories as forms of fixed "territory," the latter being consumed by the former.[11] Thus, seeking to destabilize what he sees as an overdetermined and unidirectional relationship between text and world, Williams emphasizes that the scripture is not a "clear and readily definable territory," but is, rather, "an *historical* world in which meanings are discovered and recovered in action and

---

10. Williams, *On Christian Theology*, 142–43.

11. Williams, *On Christian Theology*, 29–43. See similar critiques made by Tanner, *Theories of Culture*; DeHart, *Trial of the Witnesses*.

encounter."[12] The Church is both guided by and interrogated by the text, and thus, lives each new moment as a potential discovery of itself and the world along this "edge." Thus, on the one hand, this intersection of Church/World is "a generative moment in which there may be a *discovery* of what the primal text may become (and so of what it *is*) as well as a discovery of the world."[13] But on the other hand, it is also a moment of discovery for the Church itself, regarding itself: "the interpretation of the world 'within the scriptural framework' is intrinsic to the *Church's* critical self-discovery. . . . In judging the world, by its confrontation of the world with its own dramatic script, the Church also judges itself."[14] Williams's use of the term *generative* is helpful here, inasmuch as it makes room for the creative work of the Spirit at this critical intersection; as the Church engages the world, the Church is re-created, and discovers itself.

Consequently, Williams clarifies that the shape of the Church's proclamation to the world cannot be determined a priori: "At any point in its history, the Church needs both the confidence that it has a gospel to preach, and the ability to see that it cannot readily specify in advance how it will find words for preaching in particular new circumstances."[15] But this reticence to determine the shape of the Church's speech to the world is grounded not only in the endless diversity of contexts that constitute "world," but also in the inability to predetermine the ways in which the Church will discover itself and be shaped along that edge of engagement. So, undoubtedly for Williams, the Church enters into the work of "constructing meanings," and thus, must be involved in the broader conversations of "art and politics in the widest sense of those words."[16] But even more, what is at stake is not just the judgment of the world by the Church through the lens of the scriptural text, but also the necessary development within the Church of "a new self-identification, a new self-description, in the categories of Christian prayer and sacrament," that will be both "possible and intelligible" in each particular intersection of Church/World.[17] So conceived, it will not be wrong to describe this scenario as a kind of conversion, inasmuch as it reflects a transformation equally applicable to the discoveries made in

---

12. Williams, *On Christian Theology,* 30.

13. Williams, *On Christian Theology,* 31.

14. Williams, *On Christian Theology,* 31.

15. Williams, *On Christian Theology,* 31.

16. Williams, *On Christian Theology,* 32.

17. Williams, *On Christian Theology,* 32.

both world and Church.[18] In short, the Church is called to engage with the world in order to "*rediscover* our own foundational story in the acts and hopes of others," so that "we ourselves are converted and are also able to bring those acts and hopes in relation with Christ for their fulfillment by the re-creating grace of God."[19]

This story must be "rediscovered," of course, because the Church consistently shows the signs of having forgotten it. This is to say that, for Williams, the Church's pursuit of evangelistic mission in the world will be guided not only by the practices of discernment, but also by repentance and confession. Such confession and repentance do not undercut mission, but display the Church in mission, inasmuch as the self-corrective humility of the Christian community is in and of itself witness to the world. Yet, Williams seems to push this idea further, again in order to suggest the crucial relationship of repentance and confession as missional practices not only of the Church witnessing to the world, but of the Church's determination and identification vis-à-vis the world. For Williams, the discernment of sin in the world is also the confession of sin from within the Church, for "if it is to be itself, it has no option but to live in penitence, in critical self-awareness and acknowledgement of failure. It must recognize constantly its failing *as* a community to *be* a community of gift and mutuality, and warn itself of the possibility of failure."[20]

While this vision goes some distance toward showing us a more complicated picture of the People of the Church in relation to the world, it is still ecclesiology formed along the *via negativa*, exercising care not to overstate our speech about this particular People's identity or agency in relationship to the world. Can we say more? How shall we identify the Church when it does appear at this intersection with the world? On our way toward developing an account of ecclesial agency foundational to a Methodist expression of evangelistic mission, I continue to employ Williams, who suggests that the Church is identified less by its reflection of certain "marks," and more by its appearance as a community of gift and mutuality when engaged in the discovery of the other in forgiveness and reconciliation.

---

18. As Williams puts it, "The Christian is involved in seeking conversion—the bringing to judgement of contemporary struggles, and the appropriation of some new dimension of the transforming summons of Christ in his or her own life" (Williams, *On Christian Theology*, 33).

19. Williams, *On Christian Theology*, 38.

20. Williams, *Resurrection*, 48–49.

The Discoverability of the Church

In Rowan Williams's reflections on the terrorist attacks in the United States, *Writing in the Dust*, he suggests the vital need for a kind of vulnerable openness between peoples that he calls "breathing space." In the breathing space, Williams argues that we might

> become conscious, as people often do, of two very fundamental choices. We can cling harder and harder to the rock of our threatened identity—a choice, finally, for self-delusion over truth; or we can accept that we shall have *no* ultimate choice but to let go, and in that letting go, give room to what's there around us—to the sheer impression of the moment, to the need of the person next to you, to the fear that needs to be looked at, acknowledged and calmed (not denied). If that happens, the heart has room for many strangers, near and far.[21]

While not explicitly addressing an ecclesiological question here, Williams does point to a kind of space where the Church might also be said to "appear," not as a fixed entity, but more as an event, and even more specifically, as an event of reconciliation and forgiveness. This is the generative move toward a community where "the heart has room for many strangers."[22]

The formation of this community is not a human responsibility, at least not primarily, inasmuch as Williams roots this generativity within the relationship of giving and receiving at the heart of the Triune God, revealed in the life, death, and resurrection of Jesus. Thus, we come to see that

> God's creative act as in itself a giving away, a letting go; and because the giving away of Jesus is itself a response to the giving God whom Jesus calls *Abba,* we learn that God's act includes both a giving and a responding, that God's life is itself in movement and in relation with itself. . . . Jesus is the fleshly and historical form of God's act of giving in its responsive dimension—God's answer to God, the embodiment of God's own joy in God.[23]

This vision is centrally important to understanding Williams on the nature of the Church's relationship to the world in evangelistic mission. The nature of God, the "everlasting motion of the divine life," is the "will

21. Williams, *Writing in the Dust,* 59–60.
22. Williams, *Writing in the Dust,* 59–60.
23. Williams, *On Christian Theology,* 234.

to give," a movement captured in the creedal affirmation, "begotten of the Father before all ages."[24] God's eternal existence in the life of gift and communion finds expression in the sending of the Son into time, into history, where the Son embodies the Divine life in the "making of communion."[25] What we find in Jesus is the unique expression of God's will, a "human identity shaped wholly by the divine purpose of reconciliation through communion."[26] In Jesus, God inaugurates a new kind of "belonging together," creating a Peoplehood extended beyond the limits of Israel alone, and centered in Jesus's offer of a new community not subject to the "oppressive powers of the present world order," but opened as a new possibility for human togetherness.[27] In time, the pursuit of this reconciliation through communion, this new possibility for human togetherness, is what we call the Church.

It may already be clear why these theological commitments will not fall prey to overstating the differentiation of Church/World. While there is no question that the particular sort of "human belonging" that Jesus embodies and creates represents a vision of a particular Peoplehood "more comprehensive than any existing form of human connectedness, race, kindred, or *imperium*," it is a vision unrealized unless it continually extends itself as a possibility for human relations in the world.[28] Thus, there will be a Church, a community of the Body of Christ, only where a new social wholeness is created in the generative work of the Triune God extending the giving and receiving of forgiveness and reconciliation. This is what we see in Jesus, as the expression in time of God's inner life. As such, Jesus cannot but reveal the continual movement toward that which reflects God's very nature. In Williams's words, this is "unrestricted communion."[29] Thus, the Peoplehood of the Church is a Peoplehood always developing, always growing, extending itself to reach what one theologian has called "the other half of the reconciling event."[30]

We can also see at this point how the notion of this always-developing Peoplehood gestures toward the development of a missional, and deeply

24. Williams, *Ray of Darkness*, 223.

25. Williams, *Ray of Darkness*, 223.

26. Williams, *Ray of Darkness*, 223.

27. Williams, *Mission and Christology*, 15.

28. Williams, *On Christian Theology*, 233.

29. Williams, *Ray of Darkness*, 224.

30. Yoder, "'But We Do See Jesus,'" 55.

evangelistic, ecclesiology, inasmuch as a Church understood in the terms of "unrestricted communion" can never be seen as complete. There will be a Church, but as Williams notes, it will be "a church constantly chafing at its historical limits and failures, drawn toward the universality of communion it celebrates and proclaims in its eucharist."[31] This is the case, because this reconciliation and forgiveness proclaimed refers not to the eternal memory of the acquittal of events that reside entirely in the past, but refers, rather, to the fact that such reconciliation and forgiveness are socially located and communally embodied. This reconciliation is always being unveiled, constantly extended and discovered as persons previously separated are brought together in this holistic way.

In this light, it is unsurprising that Williams suggests that mission (and by extension, the Church's evangelism) cannot be considered outside of either the Kingdom of God or the catholicity of the Church. Because the confession of Jesus as Lord acknowledges Lordship over all creation, it is to all creation that the Church is drawn to serve in mission and evangelism. From this perspective, it becomes

> possible to see how both catholicity and mission are dimensions of the Church's form of life, a life endlessly sensitive, contemplatively alert to human personal and cultural diversity, tirelessly seeking new horizons in its own experience and understanding by engaging with this diversity, searching to see how the gospel is to be lived and confessed in new and unfamiliar situations; and doing this because of its conviction that each fresh situation is already within the ambience of Jesus' cross and resurrection, open to his agency, under his kingship.[32]

The Church surely exists in a distinct way vis-à-vis the world, enacting a relationship that helps to constitute mission—but mission cannot be separated from catholicity, Williams argues. The cooperative movement of mission and catholicity means that the "incalculable variety of human concerns can be 'at home' in and with the confession of faith in Jesus."[33] Consequently, catholicity and mission aim "only to keep open and expanding the frontiers of the community of gift" and the extension of unrestricted communion.[34]

31. Williams, *Ray of Darkness*, 224.
32. Williams, *Resurrection*, 56–57.
33. Williams, *Resurrection*, 57.
34. Williams, *Resurrection*, 57.

For Williams, the movement that describes the missionary community also describes a sacramental community. Williams will say that the goal for the extension of this unrestricted communion is the creation of a "visible community, the tangible reality of the sacramental fellowship that is entrusted with the communication of the good news," a description which again suggests a community with density.[35] However, the offer of the sacramental life is not the offer of the gift of Jesus as if he were a possession of the Church to give. Rather, the Church's liturgy is itself a leaning in both ways, as it is at once a witness to the world of the Church's "continuity" with the community that bears his name, as well as a sign of the Church's "awareness" that it has not "mastered" Jesus, and accordingly, Williams writes, "never shall, since it is always [Jesus] who continues to invite, in the pulpit, or at the table or at the font."[36]

This is why the Church as a People must engage the world, in Williams's terms, "open to judgment." The Church embodies an evangelical stance in relation to the world as a sacramental community that leans both ways. The Church practices discernment, engaging memory, history, confession, and repentance not as an intra-ecclesial practice, or as an individualized spiritual discipline, but instead, as openness to the many places, peoples, and stories through which God communicates judgment and generates the possibility of "unrestricted communion."[37] Evangelistic mission, then, can only be the constant movement of the Church from the memory of its past to the interrogation of its present, and from repentance of its sin to the world of "division and competition" within which the offer of the unrestricted communion of the Trinitarian life, reflected and enacted first in Jesus and now in his body, can be discovered as *good news*.

Ecclesial Agency: Evangelism as Intercession

We can learn, from Rowan Williams, to envision the Church's agency in an ongoing engagement with the world in evangelistic mission as a kind of "intercession." In "Being a People: Reflections on the Concept of the 'Laity,'"[38] Williams examines the priestly vocation of the people of God in

35. Williams, *Mission and Christology*, 20.

36. Williams, *Mission and Christology*, 21.

37. Williams writes, "Only a penitent Church can manifest forgiven-ness" (Williams, *Resurrection*, 46).

38. Williams, "Being a People," 11–21.

Church/World by framing it as the calling to practice "intercession" with others in the world, and with God. He begins by drawing from the insights of William Stringfellow and Dumitru Staniloae to suggest that "before ever we ask what 'the laity' can or should be doing in the Church, we have to address the question of what the Church, the nation of the baptised, does; and this in turn depends upon having a clear answer to the question of what *Christ* does."[39] At the beginning, such a turn reflects prior conversations regarding the identity of the Church as tied to Jesus and, inevitably, to the giving and receiving of the Triune God. Recalling this sense of divine action is crucial to a developing account of the evangelistic task, because as Williams reminds us, "Without this christological and trinitarian focus, all that is said theologically about the laity is likely to reduce itself to recommendations for good works."[40]

Williams first turns to Stringfellow for the reminder that the Church describes a particular People "called above all to be a *holy* nation, exactly as was Israel, in the sense that the Church is summoned to show what a nation *might* be."[41] Not, then, a calling to holiness addressed to a select few, the vocation of the Church is to reflect the truth that all human beings are called "to belong together in justice," and thus, the Church is called to be "the priest of nations."[42] Yet, Williams is aware of the fact that such an emphasis can lead to the overstatement of the Church/World difference, so he clarifies that the Church's priestly calling is embodied in the ways in which the Church not only "shows" the world this potential, but also as it undertakes "'advocacy' on behalf of every human victim."[43] In other words, the Church must lean both ways: into the holiness of its identity, but also into the world, in a mission of advocacy.

Of course, the use of such a word as "advocacy" to describe the Church's engagement with the world may appear problematic, to the extent that it is so often used in ways entirely separated from any theological, ecclesial grounding. It is resistance to exactly this kind of severance, however, that we find in Williams's use of Stringfellow. For when the Church engages the world, and particularly when it stands with the world's victims, the Church does so as an expression of "its own experience of God's victory

---

39. Williams, "Being a People," 19.
40. Williams, "Being a People," 19.
41. Williams, "Being a People," 12.
42. Williams, "Being a People," 12.
43. Williams, "Being a People," 12.

over death . . . in conscious and articulate gratitude for God's ability to take us beyond death."[44] Consequently, such engagement cannot be defined on the world's terms, but is, Williams argues, a matter of praise and worship. Whether gathered at the table or standing with the victim, the Church is always engaged in both worship and advocacy.

This connection between worship and advocacy allows Williams to suggest that the vocation of the people of God (or, the *laos*) is best understood as a participation in the life of God in the world. In this frame, the Church is not only those "summoned to be *with* Jesus, but more significantly . . . those who are called to participate in what Jesus *does*," a role that is discovered specifically in his "givenness" or "attentiveness" to the Father.[45] This is to say that the *laos* will live a priestly life in the Church and in the world, which gives further definition to the intercessory vocation:

> Belonging to a priestly people means the absorption in one's life of the pattern of Christ's life. Utter attentiveness to the Father, an attentiveness that takes us strangely beyond any graspable picture of the divine source, demands the sacrifice of the God we can control. And as such it entails the willingness to be open to God in any and every situation, including and especially situations of apparent Godlessness. By sustaining such an openness, there is a sort of bringing of the situation to God, or at least a *naming* of the God present already. This naming and offering is the priestly task of the people, their sacrifice of praise.[46]

Recalling Williams's description of the Church considered above, we should note the ways in which this vision echoes the sense of the Church as reflecting the identity of Jesus in history, himself reflecting the ongoing giving and receiving within the divine life. In time, in its attentive relationship toward God and the world around it, the Church continues what Jesus began to cultivate: unrestricted communion.

Connecting the advocacy and worship of the Church to ongoing divine action in the world is the prelude necessary for Williams to introduce his other theological conversation partner in this article, the Romanian Orthodox theologian Dumitru Staniloae, and specifically, Staniloae's conception of the Christian's relationship with the world, described best as "responsibility." Because the People of God define their engagement with

44. Williams, "Being a People," 12.

45. Williams, "Being a People," 12.

46. Williams, "Being a People," 12.

the world within the ongoing divine action of God in the world, and among those not yet within the Church, their responsibility is to

> listen for the word of God that is there, and [then] struggle to "speak" it afresh for ourselves, drawing it into the task of shaping *human* meanings. In this sense, we make answer for creation to God; we try to "name" what is before us in such a way that God's action moves in our act and speech.[47]

However, this task is not just self-serving, for the good of the Church, but is action undertaken for the world: "*Our* response to another person is part of God's enabling of *their* response, and so of their fulfilled life."[48] Put differently, we might say that this response constitutes a sort of proclamation of the gospel that the Church enacts within the world. Again, we begin to see the connections here with an account of mission and evangelism. Yet, Williams presses further, to offer a description that goes beyond the limitations of advocacy and responsibility.

Williams brings these two theologians together in order to demonstrate the similarity of their understandings of "advocacy" and "responsibility" as forms of engagement between Church/World and, more particularly, as theological grounding for an understanding of the *laos* and their mission, an understanding that Williams finally seeks to capture in a descriptive suggestion. As he writes, "it seems that the calling of the laity is above all to *intercede*."[49] He goes on,

> To be an advocate *within* the world for the powerless and victims is inseparable from the task of representing the powerless before God. Where I stand, day by day in the world, will determine what I can and must do in the liturgy where the connections of the world and the Kingdom are woven afresh. There will be no truthful liturgy without the conscious bringing into the sphere of God's action in Christ as presented in the liturgy the knowledge that arises from where the baptised person actually stands.[50]

Such a vision of intercession undermines an overstated differentiation of Church/World, as Williams argues that the People of God are called to "represent" and to "give voice" to all human persons, "to proclaim and

47. Williams, "Being a People," 14.
48. Williams, "Being a People," 14.
49. Williams, "Being a People," 16.
50. Williams, "Being a People," 16.

honour the connection which God has already made between the world and the divine life, in creation and in redemption."[51] Thus, while baptism constitutes the citizenship of the Christian "nation," the particularity of the Peoplehood that is the Church, this nation, this People, is created explicitly for priestly presence within the world, as advocate and intercessor, "naming" God's work in the world and "bearing" it to God in work and prayer.[52]

As I have hinted along the way, despite the fact that the word "evangelism" does not appear within these descriptions, we can discern an account of evangelistic mission taking form here. In *Evangelism after Christendom*, Bryan Stone rightly argues that "the most evangelistic thing the Church can do today is to be the Church."[53] But in order to avoid any potential overstatement of the Church/World differentiation, I suggest that it may be helpful to think of the Church's evangelistic mission as the constant stance of living between God and the world, and constantly leaning both ways at once, bearing one to the other, articulating the work of God in the world as well as the need of the world to God. In other words, this evangelistic mission is not just to *offer* prayer, but rather, to *embody* prayer, to participate in God's ongoing creation and redemption of the world through Jesus Christ in the power of the Holy Spirit. Even more specifically, we might say that this evangelistic mission is *to intercede*. Evangelism in intercessory terms communicates the agency of the Church in, but not of, the world.

Framed in this intercessory embodiment, we can point to a way beyond the problematic tendency to under and overstatement of the Church/World difference in evangelistic mission. On the one hand, evangelism as intercession avoids problems related to the understatement of the Church/World difference, inasmuch as it insists on a thick understanding of the Church's identity, grounded in a community formed in the tradition and practices of Christian community. Williams argues that the capacity to discern God at work in the world is not imputed to the Church, but is rather a matter of formation, and more particularly, is the expression of a sacramental life lived inside and outside the Church. Because the Eucharist is the prayer that "immerses itself in God's action of self-identification with the powerless," it is both the formation for and description of a way of life for the People of God that troubles any tendency to read the relationship of

51. Williams, "Being a People," 17.
52. Williams, "Being a People," 15.
53. Stone, *Evangelism after Christendom*, 15.

Church/World in tribal or sectarian terms.[54] As Williams writes, because "the sacramental transformation is, crucially, the work of the *laos*, in its entirety, beginning in the involvement and advocacy of daily experience, the opening of situations to the articulating of God's victory," then "it is impossible to see the daily work and 'secular' identity of the baptised as matters of theological indifference: the whole must be seen as a matter of Eucharistic intercession, the making of connections."[55] The sacramental community is always leaning into God and into the world when gathered at the table for Eucharist or for a meal at the local shelter.

This vision already gestures to the ways in which this account of evangelism as intercession also counters the potential error of overstating the difference of Church/World. While the Church must always be engaged in the work of formation, Williams clarifies that it is a mistake to think about liturgy or catechesis solely as a "training to do things," with evangelism simply becoming the work of "defending or communicating the Gospel."[56] If the People of God are called to participate in the ongoing divine action, which is to say, if they are called not only to be with Jesus, but to do what

54. Williams, "Being a People," 17.

55. Williams, "Being a People," 17. This sounds quite similar to the description Randi Rashkover offers in her introduction to *Liturgy, Time, and the Politics of Redemption*. She writes, "I have, according to Barth, an obligation to the neighbor rooted in the possibility that while he may be a sign of Christ's humanity, he himself may not be privy to the Word of God. I must, therefore, say something to him about the other side of human need— namely, God. I must, in other words, say something to him about the possibility of announcing his need to God in prayer. Of course, my telling the neighbor about the God to whom we may pray is nothing more than my act of taking up his need in the content of my prayer. My testimony to God before him is occasioned by and directly related to the particularities of his need. Through my encounter with the neighbor, the Word of God has descended into the particularities of his encounter with the world. The Word of God has been invited into the outer sanctuary and herein the order of redemption partakes in the reality of the current situation, all the while the current situation is transformed into the Word of God. Of course, Barth says, I must translate and manifest my prayer for the next one in and through concrete actions. My effort to lend her assistance takes on the form of actions in the world whether these actions be political, economic, medical, legal, or moral. The Word of God extends into and changes the shape of these concrete worldly behaviors. The believer both builds the order of praise and redeems the world through the very activities that constitute its reality. Rooted in praise for God and extended into the prayer for the neighbor, these concrete forms of assurance are liturgical, through and through" (Rashkover, "Introduction," 19). From an explicitly Christian perspective, Williams clarifies these thoughts on prayer, identifying such prayer as both *intercessory* and *Eucharistic*.

56. Williams, "Being a People," 19.

Jesus does, then they are called to an ongoing openness, an "abiding" with God and the world that cannot be differentiated from their time at the Table in the Church or from their advocacy, responsibility, and intercession at home, at work, and in the streets of the world. What defines their existence is exactly that "givenness" and "attentiveness" to God that allows them to name the presence of God not only in the Church but also in the world. This means that evangelism cannot only be the Church's verbal and visual witness to the watching world. This is the case because there is no account of Church separable from the appearance of this People formed at the intersection of Christians and the "other half of the reconciling event."[57] In short, the Church must be the Church, but it can only be the Church as it is engaged in the world.

It is significant for an account of evangelism that this intercession has a practical, and we might say, a linguistic edge, described by Williams in different parts of this article as "the opening of situations to the articulating of God's victory,"[58] and "the naming of the world in and through God."[59] This characterization suggests an ongoing work of the Church in the world that may help to define its evangelistic task in ways that will not be limited to the overstated "aesthetic display" of the Church's "priestly" life, nor to the practices of understatement that give the world the lead in the adaptation and translation of the gospel and its ecclesial embodiments.

Resisting these tendencies, Williams's vision reconnects an account of evangelistic engagement of Church/World to a Christological account of God's redeeming work in Church and amidst the principalities and powers of the world. The intercessory work of the *laos* is to give voice to this unfolding redemption, so that

> the speech of the believer becomes the attempt to allow God's word to be heard, the word that is at the ground of the sufferer's being, and, by letting it be heard, to begin to weave it closer into the broad pattern of a reconciled world, where the words of created diversity are brought back into harmony with the true and single Word of God which is eternal.[60]

---

57. Yoder, "'But We Do See Jesus,'" 55.

58. Williams, "Being a People," 17.

59. Williams, "Being a People," 15.

60. Williams, "Being a People," 15. Perhaps we see such an effort embodied in the essays that constitute Williams's book, *Lost Icons: Reflections on Cultural Bereavement.*

An intercessory evangelism emphasizes the way in which the Church is always *in* the world and *for* the world, and still, fully the *Church*, always leaning both ways at once.

Implications for (United Methodist) Ecclesiology and Evangelistic Mission

In this final section, I turn to consider how this understanding of the Church as a People taking shape via an intercessory leaning in both ways has an impact on our developing Methodist ecclesiology. In the prior chapter, I drew attention to the ecclesiological significance of the General Rules in forming a visible, practicing, and witnessing Methodist People. Supporting this emphasis, we dwelt most specifically with Wesley's writing and with the practices of the disciplined communities of his early Methodist movement.

Yet, Methodism's development throughout the remainder of Wesley's life, and particularly in the centuries after his death, in both Britain and America, produces a problem for an account of Methodist ecclesiology that depends solely on the General Rules. This problem arises due to the changing shape over time of the Methodist movement, wherein Methodism moved from a collection of disciplined communities to the inclusion of various institutions such as schools, dispensaries of medical care, and eventually, the structures of a modern denominational Church. This acknowledgment leads us to widen our aperture, to see beyond the small group, the class meeting, or the modern congregation or local Church, in order to include these larger instantiations of Church in an expression of a Methodist evangelistic ecclesiology. At the same time, these expressions of Church must be called to embrace the ways in which they live within the differentiation of Church/World, always leaning both ways at once.

Instead of believing (as individual congregations may be wont to do) that they are the primary expression of the Church in the world, attaching an inappropriate solidity to their structure and mistakenly assuming that they alone bear the responsibility to carry the gospel to the world, these embodiments of Church must be subjected to the vision of Church as a People leaning both ways, formed as a sacramental community and, at the same time, discovering identity at the point of its intersection with the world. As Russell Richey has argued, "Methodism was bigger and littler than parish."[61] We seek an expression of Methodist ecclesiology that not

61. Richey, *Methodist Connectionalism*, 239.

only leans both ways between tradition and mission, or Church/World, but also between congregation and denomination, seeing evangelism as a central practice for all.

Conclusion: Connectionalism as Intercession

Pursuing this ecclesiological vision, I want to take up a key Methodist marker for ecclesiological identity: the calling to be a "connectional" Church. First, I will reflect on some of the ways in which connectionalism has been interpreted as key to Methodist ecclesiology. Second, I will consider some critique of that interpretation on the way to developing a constructive suggestion. This proposal will come, third, in an argument about the need for connectional identity as a Methodist expression of a Church in the world, but understood as an expression that embodies a Peoplehood engaging the world via an intercessory stance, fulfilling evangelistic mission by leaning both ways between God and the world, always at once.

Considered a feature (present, if not named as such) of the early Methodist movement, connectionalism (or as rendered in the British Methodist context, "connexionalism") referred to a basic set of practices and structures that sought to ensure the presence of unity, primarily among the preachers, but eventually extending as well to the general members of the Methodist societies in England. Retaining such connection was not a primary concern in the earliest days of the movement, as the visible and practical source of unity for all of Methodism lay in the one person of John Wesley; he was the one point with which all others in Methodism remained "in connection." However, as Richard Heitzenrater points out, "connexionalism" began with the preachers in the movement: "Wesley came to realize that this sense of connectedness of the preachers to him should also be strengthened by an explicit expression of covenantal relationship among themselves. . . . Therefore a covenant was drawn up in 1752 in which the preachers declared that they would speak and act in union with each other."[62] Eventually, this sense of unity spread beyond the preachers to include the members of the movement as well; as Wesley wrote to the people of Trowbridge within a year of his own death, "I have only one thing in view—to keep all the Methodists in Great Britain *one connected people*."[63] Brian Beck leads us to see Wesley's same commitment to unity focused on the fledgling American Church

62. Heitzenrater, "Connectionalism and Itinerancy," 29.

63. Richey, Campbell, and Lawrence, *Connectionalism*, 30–31 (emphasis mine).

when he quotes Wesley's last letter to the Methodists overseas. Here, he "urges them to declare clearly that 'the Methodists are *one people* in all the world [and] that it is their full determination so to continue.'"[64] It is from this desire that structures and practices develop in the Methodist movement to ensure this connectedness and unity: the structure of the Conference and the practices of Holy Conferencing. Of course, as Russell Richey reminds us, the annual conference continues in United Methodist polity as the "basic" or "fundamental" body of the Church, enjoying "that distinction constitutionally, operationally, theologically, and historically."[65]

Despite these efforts to ensure unity and common identity, as Methodism began to evolve from movement to Church, connectionalism came to describe the institutional bureaucratic structures of the Church rather than the interconnected nature of a missionary movement. Indeed, despite efforts to counter this development in more recent years, this situation has remained the same, and the "connection" is still often used in common parlance among United Methodists to refer not to the bonds of unity shared in ministry, but rather, to the structures and institutions that exist at the level of the Conference, Jurisdiction, and General Church. This is, as Richey puts it, a vision of connectionalism as "the church's officialdom, its apparatus."[66]

Countering this tendency, Methodists in Britain and in the United States have more recently paid attention to the theological commitments inherent in the connectional concept. Some focus on the explicit linkage of connectionalism to the growing awareness of the relationship of koinonia and ecclesiology developed in ecumenical theological conversation.[67] These moves were generated primarily from work at the World Council of Churches (WCC) meeting at Canberra in 1991, and particularly from the Faith and Order gathering in Santiago de Compostela in 1993, where the unity of the Church was grounded in the concept of koinonia:

> Koinonia is above all, a gracious fellowship in Christ expressing
> the richness of the gift received by creation and humankind from
> God. It is a many dimensional dynamic in the faith, life, and wit-
> ness of those who worship the Triune God, confess the apostolic

64. Beck, "Connexion and Koinonia," 131 (emphasis mine).

65. Richey, "Organizing for Missions," 99n6. See also United Methodist Church, *Book of Discipline 2016*, para. 11, 28.

66. Richey, Campbell, and Lawrence, *Marks of Methodism*, 17.

67. A significant contribution made in this conversation can be found in the work of Brian Beck, "Connexion and Koinonia," 129–41. See also Carter, *Love Bade Me Welcome*; Robbins, "Connection and Koinonia," 199–212.

faith, share in the Gospel and sacramental living, and seek to be faithful to God in Church/World.[68]

However, to go further, the report makes clear that this koinonia is not just a horizontal description of the unity shared among the visible Church in the world across space but is also descriptive of a vertical relationship; koinonia is grounded in the very nature of God as Trinity. Again, quoting from the Santiago Report:

> The interdependence of unity and diversity which is the essence of the Church's koinonia is rooted in the Triune God revealed in Jesus Christ. The Father, Son, and Holy Spirit is the perfect expression of unity and diversity and the ultimate reality of relational life.[69]

Consequently, the connection is made between the common life of members in mission and ministry within the Methodist movement and the unity displayed in the koinonia of the early Church, and both are reflective of the perichoretic inter-relations of the Godhead. To participate in the unity of the Church is to participate in the unity of God's inner life, and in this way, the "connexion" cannot be limited to a descriptive term for the structures of ecclesial organization; instead, connectionalism is given theological freight: it is the means by which Methodists are a "People" in the world, connected deeply to one another and to the Triune God who calls us together in worship and sends us out in mission.

While this move seeks to offer a theological reading of connectionalism, there has been some resistance to such an effort. In his article "Koinonia, Connexion, and Episcope: Methodist Ecclesiology in the Twentieth Century," David Chapman argues that the linking of connexion and koinonia is misguided, just to the extent that these terms are presented as in some sense interchangeable.[70] While he believes that there is something to be gained by a deeper connection between the concept of connexionalism and koinonia, Chapman does not believe that connexionalism as structural unity can be equated to the deeper and more significant unity represented by Baptism into the Body of Christ and sustained by participation in the Eucharist. "Thus it is koinonia rather than connexionalism which gets to the heart of the inward spiritual reality of Christian unity."[71] So, "whereas

68. Beck, "Connexion and Koinonia," 137.

69. Beck, "Connexion and Koinonia," 137.

70. Chapman, "Koinonia, Connexion, and Episcope," 4–10.

71. Chapman, "Koinonia, Connexion, and Episcope," 5.

connexionalism expresses the structural implications of koinonia, koinonia is the invisible reality to which connexionalism bears witness. They are the visible and invisible bonds of Christian unity."[72] With this differentiation in mind, Chapman warns against privileging connexion over koinonia, suggesting that to do this is to undervalue the greater importance of the sacramental unity that is constitutive of koinonia. He asks, "To what extent are we justified in continuing to attach greater ecclesiological significance to Wesley's network of societies than to his sacramental theology and practice?"[73] While Chapman's question does not necessarily foreclose on the possibility that such reclamation of connexionalism might be a help-ful marker of Methodist ecclesiological identity, it does remind us that we must continually attend to the ways in which Methodist identity as a "holy people" in the world is nurtured not only in our own tradition, but in the tradition of the One, Holy, Catholic, and Apostolic Church.

At the same time, Chapman's question also falls into the trap we seek to escape in this project, namely, the invitation to lean only one way. While Chapman seeks to emphasize the primacy of the theological in an evalu-ation of connectionalism, he does so in a way that requires a problematic separation of the theological from the structural. Chapman is right to the extent that the desire to read connectionalism in theological terms resists the reductionistic reading of connectionalism as solely a description of structure. But even that improved reading is subject to the critique that it may overstate that relationship, rendering it difficult to connect the vision of koinonia to the actual structures and institutions that embody Christian evangelistic mission in the world.

Richey's historical evaluation of American Methodism offers a way to conceive of the Church that leans both ways when he suggests that "Meth-odism was bigger and littler than parish."[74] On the one hand, this claim makes room for an account of Methodism that emphasizes a visible, prac-ticing, witnessing People called Methodist, nurtured by the General Rules and formed to be the Church, interceding in the world. At the same time, this claim also makes room for an account of Methodism that locates the Church in the People connected in the nexus of relationships, structures, and institutions of connectional Methodism. In this frame, connectional Methodism constitutes a basis of evangelistic engagement with the world

72. Chapman, "Koinonia, Connexion, and Episcope," 5.

73. Chapman, "Koinonia, Connexion, and Episcope," 6.

74. Richey, *Methodist Connectionalism*, 239.

that goes beyond verbal proclamation and aesthetic witness. The Church embodies an intercessory presence with "the other half of the reconciling event," seeking the extension of "unrestricted communion," in a Peoplehood that appears in the class meeting and in the General Conference and in bodies and structures, institutions and partnerships, that occur everywhere in between.

This is a claim that requires more attention. How shall we speak of the Church's evangelistic presence among this spectrum of ecclesiological location, from local to regional to global? Here, Richey leads us to consider the particularly Methodist institution of the Conference. In his book, *The Methodist Conference in America: A History*, Richey argues that American Methodists understood their Wesleyan mission "to reform the Continent, and to spread scriptural Holiness over these lands" in terms of a calling to seek "Zion," a term that "served to expand rather than limit, to place Methodism central in God's redemptive activities, to claim connection with God's people Israel and the whole of redemptive history."[75] Glimpses of this "Zion" came to pass when Methodists gathered in Conference, Richey suggests. So much more than an organizational structure or a business meeting, Methodist Conference in Richey's interpretation constituted an alternative space and time, rendering geography and temporality part of the broader eschatological frame seeking Zion. So, when Methodists gathered for Conference, whether at the level of the class, or in the regional quarterly or annual gatherings, their life together and practices with one another constituted something approximating Zion, something that they would eventually come to describe as Church.

However, it is important to note that Conference for American Methodists, particularly quarterly Conference, was not an intra-ecclesial affair. Conference was always a conglomeration of revivalist practices, and—significantly—created space and time where the People called Methodist dwelled together with the "uncommitted environment" of the "other half of the reconciling event." Richey describes this quality as the Conference's "gravitational" character. In other words, as Richey describes it, the Conference offered

> a variety of services to minister to the needs of people at different stages on the path to salvation. Under these conditions, the organization itself yielded revival—a special gravitational force exercised

75. Richey, *Methodist Conference in America*, 34.

> its pull, drew the faithful closer and dragged in new adherents, some of whom had come quite unprepared for conversion.[76]

The glimpse of Zion that appeared in the particular space, time, and gravity of the Conference, Richey argues, constituted a "new blueprint for ecclesial existence" in America.[77] The People called Methodist, whether embodied in the most local class meeting or, eventually, in the larger networks of connectional relationship, both were "in" Conference, and, we might say, "performed" Conference, and this dual location constituted what it meant to be the Church.

While these reflections on American Methodist ecclesiology are borne out of historical reflection and, for Richey, represent an argument for contemporary Methodist identity and mission, I want to extend these reflections to consider how they influence the account of evangelism taking shape here. Indeed, as Abraham has argued, evangelism is first the work of God through Christ and the Spirit, and thus, it is also the work of Christians who share in this divine *missio*. But significantly, Abraham argues, evangelism is also the work of the Church. The Church is an agent in the evangelistic task. Evangelism in these terms takes on a larger significance. It resists the separation of evangelism from mission (reductively understood), and the problematic under- and overstatement of the Church/World difference; evangelism as intercession is the work of the People of God engaging the world, and even discovering itself in that engagement. Thus, evangelism cannot be work undertaken in order to accommodate the Church to the world, nor can it be the offer only of an attractive alternative to the world.

Given our expansion of Methodist ecclesial identity to include a People in connection and conference, evangelism cannot only be the work of the congregation (or more realistically, a small portion of the congregation). While the local Church may be, as the current Discipline of The United Methodist Church suggests, the primary context for the formation of disciples, we make a mistake if we limit evangelism to this context, inasmuch as the local Church does not exhaust what we mean when we speak of The United Methodist Church. Yet, we also make a mistake if we believe that the only other option for evangelistic ministry is to locate it in the so-called parachurch, or in the ministries beyond the local Church we refer to as "extension ministries."

---

76. Richey, *Methodist Conference in America*, 34.
77. Richey, *Methodist Conference in America*, 34.

Now, intercessory evangelism is the work of the Church, which is to say, the intercessory advocacy embodied in both the class meeting practicing the General Rules as well as in the congregation, non-profit organization, and church-related school. Methodist ecclesial heritage in Class, Conference, and Connection constitutes the environment within which we can narrate a wide variety of ecclesial forms through which the People called Methodist can engage the world. In the prior chapter, I pointed to the possibility that a reclamation of the disciplined practices embodied in the General Rules could lead (and in some places is now leading) to the formation of new ecclesial community beyond the local congregation. Now, given the argument in this chapter, we can also say with renewed theological depth that the Methodist Connection also embodies the Church's intercessory vocation, standing between God and the world, practicing advocacy and responsibility and always engaging with the "other half of the reconciling event." This development gives us permission to imagine a Methodist Peoplehood taking shape through the "tactical alliances" and new partnerships with social entrepreneurs, educators, advocates, and healers, serving together in new initiatives and even institutions that offer a glimpse of the Zion at the center of American Methodist hope. All of this activity participates in the ongoing mission of God, and it can be, and has been described as, the Church's outreach, or community service, or social ethics. But I argue that beyond these terms, this work of such a People is most rightly described as *evangelism*—the intercessory stance of the People of God in the world, always leaning between Church/World, between formation and mission, between tradition and innovation, both ways at once.

Conclusion

THE DISCERNMENT NECESSARY TO determine a faithful path in the midst of the world is a task always present before the Church. Echoing Lesslie Newbigin, George Hunsberger and Craig Van Gelder claim that the Church must "encourage the encounter of the gospel with our culture," and face the fact that our task now is "learning how to be a church that by its nature lives always *between gospel and culture*."[1] The questions such a claim raises have guided this study and also point out directions for future work.

Whereas Hunsberger and Van Gelder rely on the language of culture to delineate the Church's task, I make use of the theological distinction of Church/World whose identity, agency, and relationship to each other I have articulated in order to argue that maintaining the differentiation of Church/World is a requirement for the possibility of both Christian identity and meaningful evangelistic mission. More specifically, by exploring a distinctively Methodist theology of evangelistic mission, I have argued for the Church as a Peoplehood, a politics constantly in formation, engaging the "other half of the reconciling event" and extending "unrestricted communion" as it serves an "intercessory" role, standing between God and the world. In short, this is what is meant when we say that a missional evangelism is a calling to lean both ways at once, living dialectically at the intersection of Church/World. Put differently, the possibility of the Church's evangelistic mission in the world is contingent on the formation of a holy People called Methodist, but the formation of such a holy People is itself contingent on the Church's connection to and engagement with the world.

1. Hunsberger and Van Gelder, "Introduction," in *The Church between Gospel and Culture*, xvii.

Church, World, and Wesleyan Witness

However, we must press the image of the leaning both ways to describe not only the stance the Church takes vis-à-vis the world in evangelistic mission, but also the structures that mediate this counterpoise. This task recalls Russell Richey's insight that before the development of the "local church," Methodism was both "smaller than" and "larger than" the local congregation. As an ecclesial tradition, Methodism finds its identity and agency for evangelistic mission not only when we reflect on the congregation, but also on the smaller and larger embodiments of Methodist Peoplehood, interceding in the world. This focus certainly calls for attention to the Methodist practices of "social grace" embodied in the life of the traditional class meeting, sharing accountability, support, and sacramental life together. At the same time, I have also emphasized the ways in which Methodism embodied mission in Connectional structures, through the Conference and its "gravitational" relationship to the surrounding world, as well as to the various institutions that mediate Methodist evangelistic mission—for example, in publishing, education, and health care.

We can go on from here to argue that the renewal of Wesleyan witness and Methodist evangelistic mission is not best served by drawing primary attention to its embodiment in the congregation. Instead, we must articulate Methodist ecclesial identity and agency in a way that will include congregation, but also, the bodies "smaller than" and "larger than" the local Church as expressions of Wesleyan evangelistic mission. This serves the renewal of a Wesleyan witness, grounded in the constant theological reflection of a People discerning and navigating the shape of intercessory engagement with and in the world. It welcomes the reflection on the local congregation, but it seeks to balance that reflection with theological concern for the evangelistic mission of the larger Church's engagement with the principalities and powers of the world. It envisions a wide array of instantiations of the People called Methodist in the world, leaning both ways between formation and evangelistic mission, between priestly, prophetic, and kingly presence. It embraces the paradox of being, at the same time, a People in the world and a community continually being formed in the intercessory offer of unrestricted communion.

While we must focus on the ways that evangelistic mission so framed is the pursuit located in the community and practices of the local Church, it is perhaps less clear among those who write in evangelism how this articulation of evangelistic mission is the work of both the smallest communities as well as the Church in its most general forms. This is to say, embodied as a Peoplehood interceding in the world, evangelism describes the presence and practices of the *ecclesiola* and the *ecclesia*. What might such embodiments look like?

Smaller Than the Congregation

Recent efforts to center Methodist formation on adherence to the General Rules in renewed forms of Wesleyan band and class meetings certainly stand out as key examples of a refocusing on the significance of communities smaller than the congregation.[2] Renewed focus on the Spirit's shaping of holiness of heart and life in small gatherings practicing common prayer, shared accountability, and all the means of grace is crucial to the formation of a People called Methodist.[3] These groups inside and outside the congregation offer examples of visible, practicing, and witnessing Christian community that are important not only for the formative power they yield for those who participate, but also for the invitation they offer to people hungry for meaningful connection and friendship in a time when isolation and loneliness appear to be expanding like a plague.[4]

Another notable development mentioned briefly in chapter 3 is the formation of new or "fresh expressions" of ecclesial community that stand alongside the traditional "inherited" Church embodied in denomination and congregation, constituting what is called a "mixed economy" of Church.[5] Fresh Expressions are not "congregations" in the modern sense (requiring professional leadership, multiple age-appropriate programs, facilities and buildings), but rather, are diverse gatherings of Christians and non-Christians, engaged with the particular character of their contexts, and discerning the shape of faithful ecclesial community in each place. Such reflection has led to the formation of new (or perhaps better, "fresh") forms of ecclesial community that are smaller than the congregation, but that embody the formation and witness of a Wesleyan People engaging with the world.

---

2. See Watson and Kisker, *Band Meeting*; Watson, *Class Meeting*. See also Watson, *Pursuing Social Holiness*; Henderson, *John Wesley's Class Meeting*.

3. See Thompson, *Means of Grace*.

4. Kristof, "Let's Wage a War on Loneliness."

5. Church of England, Mission and Public Affairs Council, *Mission Shaped Church*, xi. See also Carter and Warren, *Fresh Expressions*.

While these new formations of local Christian community, whether found in house church networks, new monastic communities, or other "fresh expressions" are important embodiments of Wesleyan witness, they also point to the need for deeper theological reflections on ecclesiology, mission, and evangelism. Given prior consideration of the identity and agency of the powers in the world, we must be vigilant that interest in new forms of ecclesial community not succumb to the temptation to support institutional survival and the roles bequeathed to the Church in a consumer economy more than the extension of evangelistic mission. I have tried to show the difficulty of navigating such discernment when considering the challenges of understatement and overstatement in the Church/World distinction. Faithfully navigating the discernment of the world and the contextualization of the Church requires a robust theological framework. Such a framework is provided in a Methodist missional ecclesiology that emphasizes the Church as a People practicing evangelism as intercession.

For example, in the contextualization of the Church in new communities, we will have to ask about what difference is achieved when we think about these formations not as the work of an "incarnational" evangelism, but rather, as the evangelism of an "intercessory Peoplehood." While an incarnational perspective rightly underwrites the goodness of creation and emphasizes divine initiative, it may also lead to the mistaken belief that incarnation is a repeatable event. Even if this mistake is avoided, and ecclesial innovation is engaged within an appropriate context of repentant humility, to call new Christian community development "incarnational" may still reflect the belief that the primary agent practicing incarnation is us, rather than the Triune God.

A focus on an intercessory peoplehood avoids the formation of new Christian community that bypasses necessary engagement with the tradition and practices of the Church catholic. In other words, the evangelistic extension of Christian community does not only require reflection on incarnation, but also consideration of the "body" that Christ inhabits on the other side of resurrection and ascension, namely, the Body of Christ that is the Church. This emphasis draws attention to necessary work on the doctrine of the Church in the Methodist tradition, but even more, it clarifies the need for focus on the shape of faithful contextualization inside of an ecclesiological account. The argument here suggests that a vision of evangelism at the heart of the Church's identity and agency, an intercessory

Peoplehood standing between God and the world, "leaning both ways at once" can help.

Further work must be done to connect this account of ecclesial and missional identity to the work of new ecclesial community development, whether embodied in Fresh Expressions, traditional forms of church planting, or in the development of missional communities or other types of organization that focus on practicing Wesleyan works of piety and mercy. In addition, we must also ask how the work of pastoral and lay formation attends to the development of what some call the "pastoral imagination" (or perhaps better, a "pioneering imagination") among those formed to lead congregations and new ecclesial communities in witness and service to the world.[6] The formation and extension of the Church in these new forms of "smaller" Methodist communities is crucial to the future of the evangelistic mission and the extension of a Wesleyan witness in the world.

Larger Than the Congregation

Methodist evangelism must also be embodied in forms larger than the congregation. This may seem an uncontroversial claim, inasmuch as Methodism has a long history of developing organizations and structures for the extension of ministry in the world, framing it all as part of the Methodist Connection. However, it has been less clear that such structures and organizations carry forward not only the mission of the Church, but in the terms of this book, the evangelistic witness of the Church. I have argued that the structures and organizations of the Wesleyan Connection are best understood as embodiments of a People called Methodist practicing intercession, standing between God and the world. In the practice and witness offered to the world through these diverse expressions, we find corporate proclamation of the gospel, the announcement of the Reign of God. While this can be described in many ways, given the terms developed in this book, we can also say that the work of the Connection is evangelism.

6. The important concept of "pastoral imagination" was developed by Craig Dykstra, particularly in "Pastoral and Ecclesial Imagination." See also Scharen and Campbell-Reed, "Learning Pastoral Imagination." Building on these important insights, given the ways pastoral leaders are forming new, "fresh expressions" of ecclesial community, and given the ways theological education is adapting in other contexts to shape "Pioneer Ministers" for this work, I wonder if the concept of "pastoral imagination" may need redevelopment and expansion to also reflect a "pioneering imagination."

To make such a suggestion might seem to violate the typical "taxonomy" of ecclesial organizations beyond the congregation. Inside denominational structures, various agencies and institutions specialize to serve or support particular forms of ministry. Outside the denomination, "parachurch" organizations exist as "voluntary, not-for-profit associations of Christians . . . to achieve some specific ministry or social service."[7] Inside or outside the denominational structure, evangelism is often considered to be the work of just one type of organization, still focused on the local church as the most appropriate context for evangelistic practice. Other agencies and parachurch organizations serve a wider array of interests and concerns, including education, health care, social services, and the arts, all pursuing particular needs beyond the reach of the local church.

A Wesleyan understanding of the Methodist Connection challenges these distinctions. While the Connection included the work of bands and classes, it also extended beyond society and parish to serve broader needs in the establishment of new organizations and institutions devoted to serve, to educate, and to address various social problems. As L. Gregory Jones notes, "the Wesleyan movement, originally in England and then in the United States, and increasingly around the globe, has for much of our history been a leader in social innovation and entrepreneurship."[8] For example, we could point to the establishment of the New Room in Bristol, which "became a base for running a school for the poor, for providing food and clothes to the needy, for offering free medical care to the sick, and for helping those in the nearby prison."[9] Jones notes that it was Wesleyans who started several schools that have become well known and well regarded universities, including Boston University, Duke, Emory, and Southern Methodist University.[10]

Another key example can be found in Wesley's establishment of the Kingswood School, also near Bristol, in 1746. Given Wesley's commitment to education "as a training for a life of holiness as well as academic achievement," he developed Kingswood to offer an alternative to existing establishment and dissenting grammar schools.[11] In Wesley's words, "My design in building the house at Kingswood was to have therein a Christian family,

---

7. Willmer, *Prospering Parachurch*, 201.

8. Jones, *Christian Social Innovation*, 5.

9. Trustees for Methodist Church Purposes, "New Room," para. 3.

10. Jones, *Christian Social Innovation*, 5.

11. Ryan, *John Wesley and the Education of Children*, 105.

every member whereof (children excepted) should be alive to God, and a pattern of all holiness. Here it was that I proposed to educate a few children according to the accuracy of the Christian model."[12] Certainly the history of Kingswood makes clear that the institution was not always successful in meeting Wesley's ends. It was a school that reflected its era, as historical evidence suggests that Wesley's approach in the school did not succeed to overcome established distinctions of class and gender.[13] Even so, there is evidence that Kingswood opened its doors not only to male, but also to female students.[14] In later years, the school sought to serve the children of Methodist preachers, which required significant financial support from the Conference given the higher financial need such families presented.[15]

More to the point, what we can see in the Kingswood School is the blurring of the lines sometimes drawn between the work of the Church and the parachurch. The school's task was always, at once, evangelistic and educational, or as noted earlier, "training for a life of holiness as well as academic achievement."[16] While the Church's establishment in Wesley's context complicates the comparison, it would be difficult to articulate a strong distinction between the evangelistic mission of the Methodist society and the evangelistic mission of the Kingswood School, or of the New Room, for that matter. The point is that each of these instantiations of Methodist Peoplehood existed to serve the extension of the Church's witness in the world, in forms that are both smaller than and larger than what we might refer to now as the local church. Put differently, these examples serve together, along with many other embodiments, as the Methodist Connection, understood not solely or primarily as an organizational or institutional relationship, but rather, as a diverse set of expressions of one intercessory evangelistic mission.

12. John Wesley, quoted in Ryan, *John Wesley and the Education of Children*, 105–6.

13. Ryan argues that "rather than offering anything new" the Kingswood school "in many ways conformed to eighteenth-century norms" regarding the roles of parents, children, and education (Ryan, *John Wesley and the Education of Children*, 121).

14. A. G. Ives notes that "it may come as a surprise to the reader to learn that girls as well as boys were taken, but such was in fact the case" (Ives, *Kingswood School*, 39). An amended set of rules and curricular plans existed for girls, and they were boarded in a different house than were the boys. Even so, Ryan notes that only "a small number of girls were admitted to Kingswood School in the early years" (Ryan, *John Wesley and the Education of Children*, 107).

15. Ryan, *John Wesley and the Education of Children*, 130.

16. Ryan, *John Wesley and the Education of Children*, 105.

An Intercessory People Called Methodist:
Leaning Both Ways at Once

What might an intercessory evangelism look like, assuming it is both smaller than and larger than the local church? I find an interesting example in the "Changemaker Initiative" at the Los Altos United Methodist Church in California's Silicon Valley, led by my friend, Dr. Kim Jones. By its own description the Changemaker Initiative is "an experiment in pioneering a new kind of Church: connecting the compassion of Jesus with the skills of social innovation."[17] Here, "social innovation" refers to forms of action seeking the "good of others in a sustainable way," utilizing the skills of "teamwork, leadership, creative problem-solving, and . . . empathy."[18] Partnered with Ashoka, a long-standing secular organization engaged in social innovation and entrepreneurship, the Changemaker Initiative at Los Altos began with twenty five "Fellows" from the congregation who pitched projects to address challenges and to seek the good of others in four areas: the Church, the local community, in families, and in schools or workplaces.

What happened next was remarkable. Projects formed that drew together teams of congregants and other supporters to address a diverse array of challenges and to create sustainable solutions to improve the lives of foster children, unhoused LBGTIA youth, military veterans, and the incarcerated (just to name a few). Various ventures sought to reduce gun violence, to battle loneliness and strengthen intergenerational relationships, to stop human trafficking, and to encourage healthy uses of technology. A few even sought to extend the change-making work to the broader Church, creating pathways to share this model of faith-based social innovation with other congregations seeking to lean more definitively into their intercessory calling.

It might be said that these projects simply constitute diverse examples of congregational mission or outreach programming and must be considered separately from the proclamation and discipleship formation more clearly associated with a traditional understanding of evangelistic mission. But to be clear, the Changemaker Fellows understand their work as expressions of Christian commitments at work. As L. Gregory Jones notes, the Wesleyan movement had long practiced the establishment of social initiatives to support education, health care, and other social needs,

17. Los Altos United Methodist Church, "Changemaker Initiative."
18. Los Altos United Methodist Church, "Changemaker Initiative."

understanding such work as a "Wesleyan vision of Christian witness."[19] In the terms of this book, such Christian witness might also be described as a form of intercessory presence, the People called Methodist, practicing evangelism.

Reflecting on her experience as a Changemaker Fellow, Caryn Cranston suggested that her service clearly did not reflect a limited vision for the work of evangelism, if evangelism is best understood as the work of "directing (and sometimes seemingly bullying) people to the list of all the things they need to do and be to be God's chosen in the world."[20] Instead, she found in her experience the opportunity to speak "directly to how my life has been shaped and reconciled and reformed and now serves to help others as I accepted God's invitation to allow Jesus into mine." Engaging in this work offered through her life and witness "a living narrative of God in the world . . . a truth which simply cannot be ignored or denied as God's presence is evidenced again and again throughout the ongoing being of my life."[21]

The Changemaker Initiative connects "personal transformation (from God) with social transformation (changing the world) in a new way, fulfilling our mission as a church in a more robust, relevant, and impactful way."[22] Again, given the frames developed in this book, I would describe the Changemakers as a "People," Methodists formed in the means of grace, visible, practicing, and witnessing, embodying and engaging others through an "intercessory" presence in the world that we can call evangelism.

If evangelism can describe the intercessory presence of the Church in the world, then we must be open to the many forms such intercessory ecclesial practice might take. The diverse embodiments formed through the Changemaker Initiative makes this clear. In this light, there cannot be a limitation of evangelism to the local church, nor a sustained bifurcation of the Church's witness in the world in the categories of local versus parachurch organization, ministry, and witness. Instead, alongside the congregation, missional communities and Fresh Expressions as well as large-scale faith-based organizations and parachurch ministries must all be understood first as the Church practicing evangelism, the People called Methodist sent to intercede, standing between God and the world, always leaning both ways at once.

19. Jones, *Christian Social Innovation*, 6.

20. Cranston quoted in personal correspondence with Dr. Kim Jones, October 2019.

21. Cranston quoted in personal correspondence with Dr. Kim Jones, October 2019.

22. Los Altos United Methodist Church, "Changemaker Initiative."

Bibliography

Abraham, William. *The Logic of Evangelism*. Grand Rapids, MI: Eerdmans, 1989.

———. "On Making Disciples of the Lord Jesus Christ." In *Marks of the Body of Christ*, edited by Carl Braaten and Robert Jenson, 150-66. Grand Rapids, MI: Eerdmans, 1999.

Alper, Becka A. "From the Solidly Secular to Sunday Stalwarts: A Look at Our New Religious Typology." *Factank: Pew Research Center*, August 29, 2018. Online. https://www.pewresearch.org/fact-tank/2018/08/29/religious-typology-overview.

Arias, Mortimer. *Announcing the Reign of God: Evangelization and the Subversive Memory of Jesus*. Lima, OH: Academic Renewal, 2001.

"Ashes to Go: Taking Church to the Streets." *Ashes to Go* (blog). Online. https://ashestogo.org.

Barth, Karl. *Church Dogmatics*. Vol. 4/3.1. Edited by G. W. Bromiley and T. F. Torrance. New York: T & T Clark, 2007.

Bebbington, David. "Methodism and Culture." In *The Oxford Handbook of Methodist Studies*, edited by William Abraham and James Kirby, 712-29. Oxford: Oxford University Press, 2009.

Beck, Brian. "Connexion and Koinonia: Wesley's Legacy and the Ecumenical Ideal." In *Rethinking Wesley's Theology for Contemporary Methodism*, edited by Randy Maddox, 129-41. Nashville: Abingdon, 1998.

Bence, Clarence. "Salvation and the Church: The Ecclesiology of John Wesley." In *The Church: An Inquiry into Ecclesiology from a Biblical Theological Perspective*, edited by Melvin E. Dieter and Daniel N. Burg, 297–317. Wesleyan Theological Perspectives 4. Anderson, IN: Warner, 1984.

Berkhof, Hendrik. *Christ and the Powers*. Scottdale, PA: Herald, 1962.

Bosch, David. *Transforming Mission: Paradigm Shifts in Theology of Mission*. Maryknoll, NY: Orbis, 1991.

Braaten, Carl E. *The Flaming Center: A Theology of Christian Mission*. Philadelphia: Fortress, 1977.

Bryant, Andy. "An Invitation to Some Serious Fun." *Norwich Cathedral* (blog), January 28, 2019. Online. https://www.cathedral.org.uk/about/blog/detail/our-blog/2019/01/28/Seeing-it-Differently-blog.

Campbell, Charles. *The Word Before the Powers: An Ethic of Preaching*. Louisville, KY: Westminster John Knox, 2002.

Carter, David. *Love Bade Me Welcome: A British Methodist Perspective on the Church.* Peterborough, UK: Epworth, 2002.

Chapman, David M. "Koinonia, Connexion, and Episcope: Methodist Ecclesiology in the Twentieth Century." In *Methodism Across the Pond: Perspectives Past and Present on the Church in Britain and America*, edited by Richard Sykes, 4–10. Oxford: Applied Theology, 2005.

Chapman, Stephen B., and Laceye C. Warner. "Jonah and the Imitation of God: Rethinking Evangelism and the Old Testament." *Journal of Theological Interpretation* 2.1 (2008) 43–69.

Chaves, Mark. "The Decline of American Religion?" The Association of Religion Data Archives, 2011. Online. http://www.thearda.com/rrh/papers/guidingpapers/Chaves.asp.

Chilcote, Paul. "Evangelism in the Methodist Tradition." In *T & T Clark Companion to Methodism*, edited by Charles Yrigoyen Jr., 221–39. New York: T & T Clark, 2010.

Cobb, John B. *Grace and Responsibility: A Wesleyan Theology for Today.* Nashville: Abingdon, 1995.

———. *Is It Too Late? A Theology of Ecology.* Beverly Hills, CA: Benziger, Bruce & Glencoe, 1972.

———. *Sustainability: Economics, Ecology, and Justice.* Maryknoll, NY: Orbis, 1992.

Collins, Kenneth J. *The Theology of John Wesley: Holy Love and the Shape of Grace.* Nashville: Abingdon, 2007.

Conger, George. "Are Ashes to Go a Protestant no-no?" *GetReligion* (blog), February 14, 2013. Online. https://www.patheos.com/blogs/getreligion/2013/02/are-ashes-to-go-a-protestant-no-no.

Conklin-Miller, Jeffrey. "'Peoplehood' and the Methodist Revival." *Wesleyan Theological Journal* 46.1 (2011) 163–82.

Cray, Graham. *The Mission-Shaped Church: Church Planting and Fresh Expressions of Church in a Changing Context.* London: Church House, 2009.

Dawn, Marva. *Powers, Weakness, and the Tabernacling of God.* Grand Rapids, MI: Eerdmans, 2001.

DeHart, Paul J. *The Trial of the Witnesses: The Rise and Decline of Postliberal Theology.* Malden, MA: Blackwell, 2006.

Dykstra, Craig. "Pastoral and Ecclesial Imagination." In *For Life Abundant: Practical Theology, Theological Education, and Christian Ministry*, edited by Dorothy C. Bass and Craig Dykstra, 41–61. Grand Rapids: Eerdmans, 2008.

Hauerwas, Stanley. "Foreword." In *Toward a Theology of Evangelism*, by Julian Hartt. Eugene, OR: Wipf and Stock, 2006.

Heaney, Seamus. *The Redress of Poetry.* New York: Farrar, Straus and Giroux, 1995.

Heath, Elaine, and Scott Kisker. *Longing for Spring: A New Vision for Wesleyan Community.* Eugene, OR: Pickwick, 2010.

Heitzenrater, Richard P. "Connectionalism and Itinerancy: Wesleyan Principles and Practice." In *Connectionalism: Ecclesiology, Mission, and Identity*, edited by Dennis M. Campbell, William B. Lawrence, and Russell E. Richey, 23–38. United Methodism and American Culture 1. Nashville: Abingdon, 1997.

———. "Wesleyan Ecclesiology: Methodism as a Means of Grace." In *Orthodox and Wesleyan Ecclesiology*, edited by S. T. Kimbrough Jr., 119-28. New York: Saint Vladimir's Seminary, 2007.

Henderson, David Michael. *John Wesley's Class Meeting: A Model for Making Disciples.* Nappanee: Evangel, 1997.

Hunsberger, George, and Craig Van Gelder, eds. *The Church Between Gospel and Culture: The Emerging Mission in North America.* Grand Rapids: Eerdmans, 1997.

Hunter, George G., III. *How to Reach Secular People.* Nashville: Abingdon, 1992.

———. *Radical Outreach: The Recovery of Apostolic Ministry and Evangelism.* Nashville: Abingdon, 2003.

———. *To Spread the Power: Church Growth in the Wesleyan Spirit.* Nashville: Abingdon, 1987.

Ives, A. G. *Kingswood School in Wesley's Day and Since.* London: Epworth, 1970.

Jackson, Jack. *Offering Christ: John Wesley's Evangelistic Vision.* Nashville: Kingswood, 2017.

Job, Rueben P. *Three Simple Rules: A Wesleyan Way of Living.* Nashville: Abingdon, 2007.

Jones, L. Gregory. *Christian Social Innovation: Renewing Wesleyan Witness.* Nashville: Abingdon, 2016.

———. "The Practice of Christian Governance." *Journal of Religious Leadership* 1.1 (2002) 101–21.

Jones, L. Gregory, and Michael G. Cartwright. "Vital Congregations: Toward a Wesleyan Vision for the United Methodist Church's Identity and Mission." In *The Mission of the Church in Methodist Perspective,* edited by Alan G. Padgett, 85-120. Lewiston, NY: Edwin Mellen, 1992.

Jones, Scott J. *The Evangelistic Love of God and Neighbor: A Theology of Witness and Discipleship.* Nashville: Abingdon, 2003.

Kenneson, Phil. "Selling [Out] the Church in the Marketplace of Desire." *Modern Theology* 9 (1993) 319–418.

———. "Visible Grace: The Church as God's Embodied Presence." In *Grace Upon Grace, Essays in Honor of Thomas A. Langford,* edited by Robert K. Johnson, L. Gregory Jones, and Jonathan R. Wilson, 169–79. Nashville: Abingdon, 1999.

Kristof, Nicholas. "Let's Wage a War on Loneliness." *New York Times,* November 9, 2019. Online. https://www.nytimes.com/2019/11/09/opinion/sunday/britain-loneliness-epidemic.html.

Lipka, Michael. "A Closer Look at America's Rapidly Growing Religious 'Nones.'" *Factank: Pew Research Center,* May 13, 2015. Online. https://www.pewresearch.org/fact-tank/2015/05/13/a-closer-look-at-americas-rapidly-growing-religious-nones.

Los Altos United Methodist Church. "The Changemaker Initiative." *Changemaker Initiative,* 2019. Online. https://thechangemakerinitiative.org.

Maddox, Randy. *Responsible Grace: John Wesley's Practical Theology.* Nashville: Kingswood, 1994.

———. "Social Grace: The Eclipse of the Church as a Means of Grace in American Methodism." In *Methodism in its Cultural Milieu,* edited by Tim Macquiban, 131–60. Oxford: Applied Theology, 1994.

———. "Wesley's Prescription for Making Disciples of Jesus Christ: Insights for the Twenty-First-Century Church." *Quarterly Review* 23.1 (2003) 15-28.

Meadows, Philip R. "Anabaptist Leanings of a 'Kinda' Methodist." *Inspire Movement,* August 2019. Previously published in 2006. Online. https://inspiremovement.org/downloads/anabaptist-leanings.

Miller, Vincent J. *Consuming Religion: Christian Faith and Practice in a Consumer Culture.* New York: Continuum, 2005.

Oh, Gwang Seok. "John Wesley's Ecclesiology: A Study in its Sources and Development." PhD diss., Southern Methodist University, 2006.

Outler, Albert. "Do Methodists Have a Doctrine of the Church?" In *The Doctrine of the Church*, edited by Dow Kirkpatrick, 11–28. 1962. Reprint, Nashville: Epworth, 1964.

———. *Evangelism in the Wesleyan Spirit*. Nashville: Tidings, 1971.

Peachy, Paul. "Toward an Understanding of the Decline of the West." In *The Roots of Concern: Writings on Anabaptist Renewal 1952–1957*, edited by Virgil Vogt, 5–28. Eugene, OR: Cascade, 2009.

Powell, Luke. "Cathedral Faces Criticism for Helter Skelter Installation—But What Do You Think?" *Eastern Daily Press*, August 8, 2019. Online. https://www.edp24.co.uk/news/norwich-cathedral-helter-skelter-criticism-1-6207220.

Rashkover, Randi. "Introduction: The Future of the Word and the Liturgical Turn." In *Liturgy, Time, and the Politics of Redemption*, edited by Randi Rashkover and C. C. Pecknold, 1–25. Radical Traditions. Grand Rapids, MI: Eerdmans, 2006.

Richey, Russell. *The Methodist Conference in America: A History*. Nashville: Kingswood, 1996.

———. *Methodist Connectionalism: Historical Perspectives*. Nashville: General Board of Higher Education and Ministry, The United Methodist Church, 2009.

———. "Organizing for Missions: A Methodist Case Study." In *The Foreign Missionary Enterprise at Home: Explorations in North American Cultural History*, edited by Daniel H. Bays and Grant Wacker, 75–79. Tuscaloosa: University of Alabama Press, 2003.

Richey, Russell, Dennis M. Campbell, and William Benjamin Lawrence. *Connectionalism: Ecclesiology, Mission, and Identity*. Vol. 1 of *United Methodism and American Culture*. Nashville: Abingdon, 1997.

———. *Marks of Methodism: Theology in Ecclesial Practice*. Vol. 5 of *United Methodism and American Culture*. Nashville: Abingdon, 2005.

Robert, Dana. *Evangelism as the Heart of Mission*. Mission Evangelism Series 1. New York: General Board of Global Ministries, The United Methodist Church, 1997.

Robert, Dana, and Douglas Tzan. "Traditions and Transitions in Mission Thought." In *The Oxford Handbook of Methodist Studies*, edited by William Abraham and James Kirby, 431–48. Oxford: Oxford University Press, 2009.

Runyon, Theodore. *The New Creation: John Wesley's Theology Today*. Nashville: Abingdon, 1998.

Rutba House, ed. *School(s) for Conversion: 12 Marks of a New Monasticism*. Eugene, OR: Cascade, 2005.

Ryan, Linda A. *John Wesley and the Education of Children: Gender, Class, and Piety*. New York: Routledge, 2017.

Schmidt, Jean Miller. *Souls or the Social Order: The Two-Party System in American Protestantism*. Chicago Studies in the History of American Religion 18. Brooklyn, NY: Carlson, 1991.

Shaffer, Josh. "Too Busy for Church? Get Ash Wednesday Ashes To Go." *The News and Observer*, March 1, 2017. Online. https://www.newsobserver.com/living/religion/article135769578.html.

Sniffen, Michael. "Ashes to Go or Not to Go, That Seems to Be the Question." *Episcopal News Service*, March 3, 2014. Online. https://www.episcopalnewsservice.org/pressreleases/ashes-to-go-or-not-to-go-that-seems-to-be-the-question.

Snyder, Howard. "Pietism, Moravianism, and Methodism as Renewal Movements: A Comparative and Thematic Study." PhD diss., University of Notre Dame, 1983.

———. "The World Through a Wesleyan Lens." In *Yes in Christ: Wesleyan Reflections on Gospel, Mission, and Culture*, 15–37. Tyndale Studies in Wesleyan History and Theology. Toronto: Clements Academic, 2011.

Specia, Megan. "God Save the Cathedral? In England, Some Offer Mini Golf or Giant Slide." *New York Times*, August 13, 2019. Online. https://www.nytimes.com/2019/08/13/world/europe/uk-norwich-cathedral.html.

Stone, Bryan. *Evangelism after Christendom: The Theology and Practice of Christian Witness*. Grand Rapids, MI: Brazos, 2007.

Stringfellow, William. *An Ethic for Christians and Other Aliens in a Strange Land*. 1973. Reprint, Eugene, OR: Wipf and Stock, 2004.

———. *Free in Obedience*. 1964. Reprint, Eugene, OR: Wipf and Stock, 2006.

Tanner, Kathryn. *Theories of Culture: A New Agenda for Theology*. Minneapolis: Fortress, 1997.

Thomas, Norman E. "Ecumenical Directions in Evangelism: Melbourne to San Antonio." *Journal of the Academy for Evangelism in Theological Education* 5 (1989-1990) 149–61.

Thompson, Andrew C. *The Means of Grace: Traditioned Practice in Today's World*. Franklin: Seedbed, 2015.

Trustees for Methodist Church Purposes. "The New Room (John Wesley's Chapel)." *Methodist Heritage*, 2013. Online. http://www.methodistheritage.org.uk/thenewroom.htm.

The United Methodist Church. *The Book of Discipline of The United Methodist Church, 2004*. Nashville: United Methodist, 2004.

———. *The Book of Discipline of The United Methodist Church, 2008*. Nashville: United Methodist, 2008.

———. *The Book of Discipline of The United Methodist Church, 2016*. Nashville: United Methodist, 2016.

Van Gelder, Craig, and Dwight J. Zscheile. *The Missional Church in Perspective: Mapping Trends and Shaping the Conversation*. Grand Rapids: Baker Academic, 2011.

Warner, Laceye. *Saving Women: Retrieving Evangelistic Theology and Practice*. Waco: Baylor University Press, 2007.

Watson, David Lowes. "Aldersgate Street and the *General Rules*: The Form and Power of Methodist Discipleship." In *Aldersgate Reconsidered*, edited by Randy Maddox, 33–47. Nashville: Kingswood/Abingdon, 1990.

———. "Class Leaders and Class Meetings: Recovering a Methodist Tradition for a Changing Church." In *Doctrines and Discipline*, edited by Dennis M. Campbell, William B. Lawrence, and Russell E. Richey, 245–64. United Methodism and American Culture 3. Nashville: Abingdon, 1999.

Watson, Kevin, and Scott Kisker. *The Band Meeting: Rediscovering Relational Discipleship in Transformational Community*. Franklin: Seedbed, 2017.

———. *Pursuing Social Holiness: The Band Meeting in Wesley's Thought and Popular Methodist Practice*. Oxford: Oxford University Press, 2014.

Weil, Simone. *Gravity and Grace*. New York: Putnam and Sons, 1952.

Wells, Samuel. *God's Companions: Reimagining Christian Ethics*. Malden, MA: Blackwell, 2006.

Wesley, John. *The Bicentennial Edition of the Works of John Wesley*. Edited by Frank Baker, Richard P. Heitzenrater, and Randy L. Maddox. 35 vols. (projected). Nashville: Abingdon, 1984–.

———. "Large Minutes." In vol. 8 of *The Works of the Rev. John Wesley, MA*, edited by Thomas Jackson, 299–338. 3rd ed. Grand Rapids: Baker, 1979.

———. *The Letters of the Rev. John Wesley*. Edited by John Telford. 8 vols. London: Epworth, 1931.

Williams, Rowan. "Being a People: Reflections on the Concept of the 'Laity.'" *Religion, State, and Society* 27 (1999) 11–21.

———. "God's Mission and Ours in the Twenty-First Century." *Dr. Rowan Williams, 104th Archbishop of Canterbury*, June 9, 2009. Online. http://aoc2013.brix.fatbeehive.com/articles.php/779/gods-mission-and-ours-in-the-21st-century.

———. *Lost Icons: Reflections on Cultural Bereavement*. Edinburgh: T & T Clark, 2000.

———. *Mission and Christology: J. C. Jones Memorial Lecture*. Brynmawr: Welsh Members Council, Church Missionary Society, 1994.

———. *On Christian Theology*. Malden, MA: Blackwell, 2000.

———. *A Ray of Darkness: Sermons and Reflections*. Cambridge, MA: Cowley, 1995.

———. *Resurrection: Interpreting the Easter Gospel*. Rev. ed. Cleveland, OH: Pilgrim, 2002.

———. "The Richard Dimbleby Lecture 2002." *Dr. Rowan Williams, 104th Archbishop of Canterbury*, December 19, 2002. Online. http://aoc2013.brix.fatbeehive.com/articles.php/1808/the-richard-dimbleby-lecture-2002.

———. *Writing in the Dust: After September 11*. Grand Rapids, MI: Eerdmans, 2002.

Willmer, Wesley K. *The Prospering Parachurch: Enlarging the Boundaries of God's Kingdom*. San Francisco: Jossey Bass, 1998.

Yeago, David. "Messiah's People: The Culture of the Church in the Midst of the Nations." *Pro Ecclesia* 6.1 (1997) 146–71.

Yoder, John Howard. *Body Politics: Five Practices of the Christian Community before the Watching World*. Scottdale, PA: Herald, 2001.

———. "'But We Do See Jesus': The Particularity of Incarnation and the Universality of Truth." In *The Priestly Kingdom, Social Ethics as Gospel*, by John Howard Yoder, 46–62. Notre Dame, IN: University of Notre Dame Press, 1984.

———. "A People in the World." In *The Royal Priesthood: Essays Ecclesiological and Ecumenical*, edited by Michael G. Cartwright, 65–101. Scottdale, PA: Herald, 1998.

———. *The Politics of Jesus*. Grand Rapids, MI: Eerdmans, 1998.

Index